Abortion
in
Northern Ireland:

The Report
of an International Tribunal

The Northern Ireland
Abortion Law Reform Association

Beyond the Pale Publications

First published 1989
by
Beyond the Pale Publications
7 Winetavern Street
Belfast BT1 1JQ

ISBN 0 9514229 1 X (pbk)

Printed by:
Express Litho Ltd.
Belfast
Typeset at Oxford University Computing Service

Abortion
in
Northern Ireland:

The Report
of an International Tribunal

The Northern Ireland
Abortion Law Reform Association

Beyond the Pale Publications

Contents

List of Illustrations ii

Preface iv

1. **Introduction: Extending the 1967 Abortion Act to Northern Ireland** 1
   Abortion Law in Britain and the Irish Republic 2
   The International Tribunal on Abortion 5
   Feedback 7
   The Contents 10
   Conclusion 11

2. **The Campaign for Legal Abortion in Northern Ireland** 13
   Introduction 13
   The First Northern Ireland Abortion Law Reform
     Association 13
   The Northern Ireland Abortion Campaign 15
   The Northern Ireland Abortion Law Reform
     Association (number two) 17
   NIALRA's Survey of Political Parties 20
   NIALRA's Survey of Health Professionals and
     Advice Workers 21
   The Assembly Debate on Abortion, 1984 25

3. **Referral and Support Groups** 31
   The Ulster Pregnancy Advisory Association and the
     Family Planning Association 31
   Open Line Counselling 35
   Union of Students in Ireland 36
   The British Pregnancy Advisory Service 37
   Liverpool Abortion Support Service 41
   The Irish Women's Abortion Support Group 42

4. **Women's Groups** 44
   Introduction 44
   The Well Woman Centre 44
   The Northern Ireland Women's Rights Movement 45
   Rape and Incest Line 45
   The Rape Crisis Centre 46
   Lesbian Line 46
   Conclusion 47

5. **Women Speaking** 49
   Introduction 49
   Witness A 49
   Witness B 51
   Witness C 52
   Witness D 53
   Witness E 56

6. **Legal Evidence**   58
   The 1861 Offences Against the Person Act   58
   The Infant Life (Preservation) Act   60
   The Bourne Judgment   62
   The Legal Situation in Northern Ireland   63
   The European Dimension   63

7. **Medical Evidence**   67
   Introduction   67
   Guidelines on Abortion for Doctors in Northern
      Ireland   67
   Prenatal Diagnosis and Selective Abortion: A
      Consultant Medical Geneticist's Evidence   68
   The Lack of Routine Screening: Women's
      Experience   71
   Doctors and Abortion in Northern Ireland: A
      General Practitioner's Evidence   74
   Evidence of Dr. C. Evans, General Practitioner   77

8. **The Abortion Tribunal: The Way Forward**   80
   Statement of Panel Members   80
   Public Opposition to Abortion in Northern Ireland   82
   The Use of Law to Change Opinion   83
   How Opinion in Northern Ireland Might Otherwise
      be Changed   84
   How the Law Might be Changed in Defiance of
      Stated Opinion   85
   The Nature of Law Itself   85
   The Possibility of Defying the Law on Abortion   85
   Conclusion   87

List of Illustrations

Boxes

3.1 Common Worries and Fears of Women Seeking an
     Abortion   34
3.2 UPAA Statistics: Some Comments   34
3.3 BPAS and Office of Population Censuses and Surveys
     Statistics   40
6.1 Excerpt from the 1967 Abortion Act   58
6.2 Excerpt from the 1861 Offences Against the Person
     Act   59
6.3 Excerpts from the 1929 Infant Life (Preservation) Act   61
6.4 The European Parliament and Abortion Travel   64
6.5 Abortion and the Constitution of the Republic of
     Ireland   64

6.6   International Dimensions of Abortion Law Reform   65
7.1   Glossary of Prenatal Diagnostic Techniques   68
7.2   Glossary of Congenital Abnormality   69
7.3   The Baird Report on Infant Mortality and Handicap   71
8.1   ALRA's Statement on Abortion Law Reform   83

Tables

3.1   Percentage distribution by age groups of women having
      abortions in Britain.   40
3.2   Gestation length at time of abortion in Britain.   41
7.1   Spina Bifida Births per 1,000 Live Births, 1978-83.   72

Preface

A casual glance at Northern Ireland society could leave one believing that it is abortion-free. The law specifically outlaws abortion, and there is no mass political movement urging the changing of the law and the provision of abortion facilities. The official health statistics reveal that very few abortions are occurring in local hospitals. And over the last decade there have been relatively few deaths of women at the hands of backstreet abortionists.

But the only reason that such a harmonious picture can emerge is that Northern Ireland—like the Republic of Ireland—exports its abortions. A minimum of ten Irish women a day travel from North and South to have abortions in Britain. They do so quietly; more, given the repressive laws and attitudes in both societies, they do so secretly. Irish women *are* having abortions; they are just not having them in Ireland.

Such a fact is a damning indictment of Irish society. There is an insidious hypocrisy involved in knowing that such a large amount of 'abortion travel' occurs while refusing to acknowledge this phenomenon at the level of public debate and social policy. The debate is forced into the open occasionally, most obviously by the successful move of the Right to outlaw abortion constitutionally in the Republic of Ireland in 1984. But for the most part the major institutions of society—the law, the churches, the political parties—prefer to go their way blithely, happy that the 'problem' of abortion is not on their own doorstep.

In Northern Ireland this conspiracy of silence has been broken from time to time—by the Ulster Pregnancy Advisory Association and the Northern Ireland Abortion Law Reform Association in the 1970s and by the Northern Ireland Abortion Campaign and the second Northern Ireland Abortion Law Reform Association in the 1980s. None of these groups would claim to be pro-abortion. What they are is pro-choice, in favour of a woman's right to be given every opportunity to choose as coolly as possible whether or not she wants a child. A necessary corollary of being pro-choice is to be open to rational discussion on the subject. There are few venues for such discussion in Northern Ireland outside of sections of the women's movement. But occasionally more public discussion has taken place—most notably in a successful meeting entitled 'Breaking the Silence' held in Belfast in February 1984. That meeting was organised by the Northern Ireland Abortion Campaign.

Three and a half years later the Northern Ireland Abortion Law Reform Association organised a two-day Tribunal in Belfast, on the 7th and 8th of October 1987. An international panel of lawyers, civil libertarians, doctors and academics heard evidence from local women, doctors, lawyers, and support and advice agencies. The hypocritical silence had been temporarily broken once again.

The Report which follows summarises the deliberations of those two days in October 1987. The Northern Ireland Abortion Law Reform Association, which organised the Tribunal, also compiled this Report, and in doing so has stayed as close as possible to the written submissions and transcripts of verbal contributions of all those who participated.

We would like to thank everyone who played a part in making the International Tribunal on Abortion an unqualified success— the nine tribunalists and the two co-chairpersons, those who gave evidence, those who listened, and those groups and individuals who provided money to enable both the Tribunal and this Report to see the light of day. Above all, we are especially grateful to those whose participation was at personal expense, financial or emotional.

The conspiracy of silence needs to be broken continually. The intention of the Northern Ireland Abortion Law Reform Association is that this Report will pay its part in doing precisely that. We offer this book as a challenge to the hypocrisy of our society and in the hope that one day any woman in Northern Ireland who for whatever reason judges she cannot continue with her pregnancy will be able to have a safe, legal and as trauma-free as possible abortion close to home.

1.

Introduction:
Extending the 1967 Abortion Act to Northern Ireland

Northern Ireland was excluded from the terms of the 1967 Abortion Act and has remained excluded ever since. However, there are many good reasons for extending the Act to Northern Ireland. It was to publicise these reasons and thus hopefully influence the decision to extend the Act that the Northern Ireland Abortion Law Reform Association (NIALRA) was formed.

1. *Women from Northern Ireland are having abortions, but they are not having them in Northern Ireland.*

   Currently over 2,000 women a year are travelling from Northern Ireland to secure abortions in Britain. Official statistics which might indicate a lower figure are based on the numbers giving Northern Ireland addresses, something many Northern Ireland women will not, for obvious reasons, do. Since 1967, at least 20,000 women have travelled to Britain for abortions and the annual figure continues to rise. At the current rate, 15 women out of every 100 will have abortions during their life.

2. *Women from Northern Ireland must pay for their abortions in England.*

   Together with travel, the total cost of the return trip is around £270. This discriminates against working class and poor women who cannot afford such a sum.

3. *Those who cannot travel must endure an unwanted pregnancy or resort to the backstreet abortionist.*

   There have been five known deaths in Northern Ireland since 1967 as a result of illegal abortions, and probably more which have been officially registered in some other form. Such deaths are now unknown in Great Britain.

4. *As a result of the legal situation, certain simple and relatively risk-free ante-natal tests, which are commonly available in Britain, are not routinely offered to Northern Ireland women.*

1

The most conspicuous of these is the Alphafeto protein (AFP) test, which the **Baird Report on Infant Mortality** recommended be an elective option for pregnant women. Such tests disclose serious congenital abnormalities in the foetus. Northern Ireland has a significantly higher rate of babies born with spina bifida and Downs' syndrome than the rest of the United Kingdom; the numbers of babies born with neural tube defects in Northern Ireland is the highest in the world.

5. *The European Parliament in 1981 proposed that abortion travel should stop.*

   It urged the European Council 'to ensure that every woman who finds herself in difficulty can obtain the necessary assistance in her own country.'

6. *The law which applies in Northern Ireland is both outdated and ambiguous.*

   The relevant legislation is the 1861 Offences Against the Person Act amended by the 1945 Criminal Justice (Northern Ireland) Act (the equivalent of the 1929 Infant Life (Preservation) Act in Britain). There are no clear and agreed guidelines concerning the application of this law. As a result, there have been serious inconsistencies in its application. Even a woman whose pregnancy is the result of rape or incest, or whose health would be seriously damaged by continuing a pregnancy, cannot be guaranteed an abortion. Doctors are frequently imposing their own religious and moral judgements upon women under the guise of complying with the law. While some abortions *are* carried out in Northern Ireland, the fear of legal reprisal leads the medical profession to disguise this practice.

7. *Women in Northern Ireland are prey to isolation, fear, condemnation and loneliness in excess of women elsewhere in the United Kingdom.*

   Because of the general social, cultural and religious background, they suffer enormous emotional and psychological distress as a result of the lack of abortion provision.

8. *In terms of the current provision for safe and legal abortions, Northern Ireland lags behind most other Western societies.*

Abortion Law in Britain and the Irish Republic

With the 20th anniversary of Northern Ireland's exclusion from the terms of the Abortion Act imminent, NIALRA decided to hold a major International Tribunal in Belfast. The intention was that a number of experts from outside Northern Ireland would hear evidence from individuals and groups, mainly from within Northern Ireland, on the consequences of the absence of legal abortion facilities locally. That evidence constitutes the bulk of this Report.

In addition it was felt that the Tribunal would have relevance in relation to occurrences both in Britain and in the Republic of Ireland. As this aspect will not figure prominently in the rest of this Report, it will be considered now.

In Britain various groups were preparing to commemorate the 20th anniversary of the passing of the Act. In doing so they were not necessarily giving unqualified support to the Act. The National Abortion Campaign (NAC), in submitting evidence to the International Tribunal, put the position clearly.

'The 1967 Abortion Act ... rests on the assumption that only inadequate women will need to use abortion, or those who are in some way unfortunate ... And yet, throughout its existence, NAC has been forced to defend this very flawed law, simply because it is the best we have at the moment and because it has undoubtedly brought benefits to women ... Despite the Act's shortcomings, it has created a new climate of opinion, where in the 1985 Social Attitudes survey half those questioned thought the abortion decision should be left to the woman concerned ... Doctors' attitudes are changing too, indeed began to change immediately after the Act was passed, with GPs much more willing to prescribe contraception to their patients than before ... Whilst we continue to fight for improvements in the law—most important of which is the removal of the 1861 Act from the statute book—we must defend what we have when it is under attack. We cannot go back to 1966.'

Within months of the Tribunal NAC members, as well as those of other groups in Britain, were fully involved in the latest attempt to 'go back to 1966', the Alton Bill. The point in relation to Northern Ireland is that we were 'back' there already. In fact, in many ways, the legal position in Northern Ireland is worse than it was in Britain in 1966. At least doctors there had a judge's decision of 1938 to help them somewhat. This came out of a case where a doctor, Alex Bourne, performed an abortion and then presented himself to the police for prosecution. His defence was that his patient, a teenage victim of multiple rape, would be psychologically and emotionally damaged by being forced to continue with the pregnancy. The judge acquitted him, thus widening the previous definition that abortion could only be carried out in practice when the life of the mother-to-be was at risk.

In the Republic of Ireland the absence of legal abortion is even more emphatic. The law governing abortion is the 1861 Offences Against the Person Act without any qualifications from a later Infant Life Preservation Act, a Bourne judgment or an Abortion Act. In addition, a referendum to the written Constitution was passed in 1985 by a two-thirds majority. This amendment read:

'The State acknowledges the right to life of the unborn and, with due regard to the equal right to life of the mother, guarantees in its laws to respect, and as far as practicable, by its laws to defend and vindicate that right.' (Article 40.3.3.)

3

Following on this Amendment to the Constitution, the anti-abortion lobby was successful in bringing a case against Dublin counselling and support agencies. What is known as the Hamilton ruling (after the presiding judge) means that the Amendment to the Constitution has been interpreted as meaning that no information about abortion—including telephone numbers or addresses of clinics—can be publicised, even if the clinics concerned are outside the jurisdiction.

Women from the Republic have had to contend with many religious, social and cultural pressures if deciding to have an abortion. This was stressed in evidence to the Tribunal from Open Line Counselling, one of the agencies closed as a result of the Hamilton ruling.

'The Roman Catholic church claims the allegiance of up to 95% of the population of the Irish Republic and exercises considerable influence on social policy and moral opinion ... Terminating a pregnancy for other than terminal medical indications is a grevious, or "reserved", sin, according to the Roman Catholic Church, necessitating absolution from a cleric of more senior rank than an ordinary confessor ... Clearly, terminating a pregnancy has serious religious implications for such women, both at the time of the abortion and subsequently.'

In addition, in the aftermath of the Hamilton judgment, women have to contend with the deliberate suppression of relevant information to allow them to make an informed choice.

In the light of such moves against women's right to abortion in the mid-1980s in both Britain and the Republic of Ireland, it is clear that the International Tribunal could serve a number of purposes. Firstly, it could starkly illustrate to groups and individuals in Britain the consequences of going back to a position prior to the 1967 Act. Northern Ireland suppresses the issue of abortion, both in terms of debate and in actuality; the problem itself is exported. Secondly, there was the possibility of a message of support to groups and individuals in the Republic of Ireland. As became clear after the Hamilton ruling, women increasingly turned for information about abortion to groups in the North. Moreover, the possibility, however remote, of abortion reform in the North raises interesting consequences for the South. Open Line Counselling, in their evidence to the Tribunal, mentioned this point.

'There is a clear demand among women from the Irish Republic for legal abortion services, a demand currently being met in England. Such women are likely to feel more comfortable about the abortion experience were such services available in a more familiar religious, social and cultural climate. As abortion services are most unlikely to be provided in the Republic of Ireland in the foreseeable future ... an attractive alternative could lie in the availabiltiy of such services in Northern Ireland.'

The same notion was echoed by the submission of Defend the Clinics, the group set up as a result of the campaign of anti-abortionists to close

4

the counselling and support agencies, to the International Tribunal.

'The extension of the Act would reduce the real anguish of Irish women in many ways. In a time of economic difficulty, the reduced costs of travelling across the border are significantly important ... The reduction in the length of time spent travelling would reduce anxiety for those women who are forced to hide their choice to terminate. It would also make it easier to organise abortions at an earlier stage in pregnancy and to ensure more accessible after-care ... We also believe that the availability of abortion in the North of Ireland would force more open discussion of the issue in the 26 counties. It would also expose even more pointedly the farcicality of the Hamilton ruling.'

The International Tribunal on Abortion

But the main reason for the International Tribunal was in order to systematically present the evidence of the consequences for women of the continuing exclusion of Northern Ireland from the terms of the 1967 Abortion Act. In terms of documenting the situation as it exists, of revealing the added suffering imposed on women by the absence of local abortion facilities, of exposing the hypocrisy of a society which exports its abortion problem, the Tribunal was in essence to be an exercise in breaking the silence. It was not the first such exercise. However, it was the first to be carried out on such a scale.

Belfast's most expensive hotel, the Forum, was booked for two days, Wednesday 7th and Thursday 8th of October, 1987. Nine experts were invited to sit on the Tribunal and hear the evidence. By design, none of them were from Northern Ireland. However, all were people with a particular expertise to assess the evidence presented. The panel members were:

Dr. Kadar Asmal
Senior Lecturer in Law at Trinity College, Dublin, former Dean of Arts (Humanities) and President of the Irish Council of Civil Liberties

Julie Grant
National Union of Students Women's Officer

Dr. Fay Hutchinson
Brook Advisory Service

Sabine Klein-Schonnefeld
Lecturer in Law and Women's Studies, University of Bremen, Federal Republic of Germany

Melanie McFadyean
author, journalist and problem page writer

Wendy Savage, FRCOG
Senior Lecturer in Obstetrics and Gynaecology

Lucy Schmitz
International Planned Parenthood Federation, Holland

Sarah Spencer
General Secretary, National Council for Civil Liberties, London
Carol Tongue
Labour Party Member of the European Parliament.

During the course of the two days, the Tribunal heard formal evidence from a large number of groups and individuals, including:

Abortion Law Reform Association, London
British Pregnancy Advisory Association
Defend the Clinics Campaign, Dublin
Family Planning Association, Belfast
Irish Women's Abortion Support Group, London
Lesbian Line, Belfast
Liverpool Abortion Support Services
National Abortion Campaign, London
Northern Ireland Abortion Campaign, Belfast
Northern Ireland Abortion Law Reform Association, Belfast
Northern Ireland Women's Rights Association, Belfast
Open Line Counselling, Dublin
Rape and Incest Line, Belfast
Rape Crisis Centre, Belfast
Ulster Pregnancy Advisory Association, Belfast
Union of Students in Ireland, Dublin
Well Woman Centre, Belfast.

As regards individuals, some are named in the Report which follows, while others, especially those women who gave private evidence on their experiences of abortion, are not. In addition, a number of people spoke from the floor either in an individual capacity or representing an organisation. Time was set aside for such interventions, most notably on the final afternoon of the Tribunal.

The evidence was grouped under five separate headings, and this is reflected in the organisation of the Report. They were:

Voluntary and Women's Groups
Pregnancy Advisory and Support Groups
Medical Evidence
Legal Evidence
Individual Experiences (private session only).

In addition, there was an opening session where the history of the campaign for abortion facilities in Northern Ireland was presented. This too forms the basis of a chapter in this Report.

That the International Tribunal was a success was evidenced by a number of factors. Firstly, it was already clear when such a representative cross-section of informed groups and individuals agreed to give evidence and such a high-powered group of experts agreed to hear that evidence that the proceedings were going to be of a very high standard. All in attendance agreed that the submissions were always informative, and often moving, and that the information presented was in some cases new to even the most seasoned of campaigners present. In addition, the panel members listened attentively and cross-examined presenters sympathetically. In no small measure the quality of presentation and cross-examination were a result of the sensitive management of the two chairpersons, Inez McCormack of the National Union of Public Employees in Belfast, and Anne Maguire, Women's Officer of the Queen's University Students' Union in Belfast.

Writing to participants afterwards, the organisers summed up their feelings about the success of the event in the following terms.

'We believe that the Tribunal was an unmitigated success. It brought together professionals and activists from Britain and from Ireland, north and south, and could be said to have been the most representative meeting ever of its kind where people have come together to discuss the issue of Irish women travelling to Britain for abortions. Furthermore, it was both informative and moving. Many people have taken the time to tell us how impressed they were by the event; we can only hope that you too were impressed. Our only frustration is in relation to the local media. We handed them on a plate a press release relating to one of the most important events of its kind in recent years in Belfast. We persuaded people of major importance to sit on the Tribunal and made sure that nothing stood in the way of them being freely available to the media for interview. For the most part, the media chose to ignore the event, not even bothering to walk the few hundred yards from their respective bases to see what was happening or to interview someone like Wendy Savage who is constantly badgered by the media in Britain for her opinions on matters to do with women's fertility and sexuality. For us the experience served to underline the fact that the media's laziness is part of the continuing conspiracy of silence in Northern Ireland in relation to abortion.'

Feedback

Some of the Tribunal members wrote afterwards of their conviction that the event was supremely successful.

Dr. Kadar Asmal, in a letter to the organisers, stated:

'I am convinced, after listening to the observations and testimony of women, doctors and lawyers in Northern Ireland, that the present position concerning abortion in the North is ambiguous, uncertain, and leaves much discretion in the hands of one or two professional people. Abortion exists in Northern Ireland for some women if they are able to persuade specialists that they come within the provisions of the Infant Life Preservation Act. Some doctors interpret this Act generously; others very restrictively. It seems to me that the issue is not whether abortion should be permitted in the North, as some politicians allege, but whether the termination of pregnancy should be regularised and be in conformity with the legislation in the rest of the United Kingdom, which is itself fairly restrictive. The arguments presented at the Tribunal were irresistible and conclusive. The legislation for Northern Ireland should have an in-built provision for advice and after-care facilities, as we were very impressed by the virtual lack of these for women who had to go to Britain from Northern Ireland for abortions. The traumas, isolation and sense of bewilderment so vividly brought to our attention by witnesses must be averted and this can only be done by adequate, publicly-funded services of advice and after-care.'

In similar vein, Dr. Wendy Savage wrote as follows:

'Listening to the women giving evidence, and reading their tragic stories, reminded me of the days before 1967 in England. Today, although the decision to end a pregnancy is still, and always will be, a difficult one for the woman, the extra shame and guilt and the loneliness which added to her burden has been lifted. In Northern Ireland, it is still there and it is compounded by the lack of any understanding by those in public positions (such as MPs) and their feeling of isolation within their own community.'

Lucy Schmitz wrote from Holland:

'I found it a very useful and well-organised meeting. I cannot measure myself the impact it has had on the media and public opinion in your country. For the women and men participating in it it certainly must have been a learning and revealing experience. So it was for me. As I told you, I was working for five years as a staff member of the Dutch Federation of Abortion Clinics, called STIMEZO-Netherlands. Fourteen clinics at that time were members of this Federation. Although I was not working in the services myself, I saw many women who visited the clinics for an abortion and heard many experiences of the health workers of those clinics. At that time, from 1978 to 1984, many women from abroad came to the Netherlands for an abortion—from West Germany, Belgium, France, Spain, Austria. What was astonishing for me was that the situation in your country was even worse than the one for the women who had to go to the Netherlands for an abortion at that time: the lack of information, the feelings of guilt, the loneliness, the lack of money, the fear and anxiety and, last but not least, the bad quality of the services. From time to time I still remember the report of the woman in the private session who told about her second trimester abortion in an English clinic and who said that the clinic personnel did not prevent her from seeing her dead foetus after a prostaglandine abortion. This is the most terrible thing I have heard and, as I understand from other panel members, this is not an exception and seems to be done on purpose. I see this as a criminal activity and I was and am very much convinced of the fact that people

8

who have moral objections against abortion cannot deal properly with the women who are looking for help. I think that this is very important for your future in which the women of Northern Ireland will and must have the possibilities to have good abortion services in their own country. I hope that this future will not be far away.'

Fay Hutchinson's lengthy reply stressed many of the factors which will be treated at length in the Report.

'I was very pleased to be invited to sit on the International Tribunal on Abortion. As a medical officer at the London Brook Advisory Centres, I was well aware of the problems facing women from both Northern Ireland and the Republic who have an unwanted pregnancy and need an abortion. Even as far away as our London centres we see a number of women who are determined to have an abortion rather than continue with the pregnancy, and have had to overcome numerous difficulties to get that far. We do not see the women with adequate resources who can get help through the private sector, but mostly the younger woman, poorly paid worker or unemployed student or housewife with no financial means, having used the money they can acquire to make the journey to England. Often because of the difficulty in raising the money, finding an excuse to visit, such as staying with a friend or relative, waiting for the school holidays, the pregnancy is more advanced, which in itself makes greater difficulty in referring for a termination. The need for an abortion at a later date adds to any risks.

I feel concerned about the welfare of women whose circumstances make referral for abortion a matter of urgency. It reduces the time in which they may be counselled before the referral, and the pressures they are under make it difficult for them to look at the negative side of the experience. Where ambivalent feelings, that most women have, of regret and sadness have not been explored, the guilt and depression after the abortion is likely to be greater. The whole climate of "illegality" in having to travel overseas adds to the tensions of a difficult time and means that the woman may not be supported by her partner, family or friends when she needs them most. I am also concerned that they have to return home quickly and lose the supervision in the post-abortion period when complications may arise.

Listening to reports and personal evidence given at the Tribunal, I felt a growing anger that women in an area that legally is a part of the UK are excluded from the provisions of the 1967 Abortion Act and are penalised if they have an unwanted pregnancy. The climate of fear and anxiety reminded me of the situation in the rest of the UK before 1967, and in the same way it is the younger, poorer, less able who are unable to get the help they desperately need who are discriminated against. The fact that at least 20,000 women have had to travel to England shows their determination to get safe, legal abortions and is evidence of the need.'

Writing in *Labour and Ireland* (number 19), Julie Grant had this to say:

'It was a gruelling two days ... Women travelled from many countries to be present or to give evidence to the Tribunal. Many organisations and individuals working in Ireland put themselves at risk by participating. It is an indictment on the press that the Tribunal and its findings were hardly reported. It is of course naive to consider the extension of the 1967 Act in isolation from the general context of the relationship between Britain and Ireland, but until such time as that situation is resolved, refusal to extend the Act is contradictory and causes widespread misery to thousands of Irish women.'

Sarah Spencer also concentrated on the media's failure in an article in *New Statesman*.

'For two days we heard moving personal testimony and disturbing evidence from doctors, lawyers and advice agencies. The fact that, twenty years after the 1967 Act, this story needed to be told, and that it was at last being told, publicly, in Belfast's premier hotel, was extraordinary. Yet it received almost no press coverage in Northern Ireland and none in Britain. While the women broke their silence, the media did not. The Tribunal has succeeded in breaking the silence. While women in Britain are preparing to defend the rights which we already have from the ravages of the Alton Bill, women in Northern Ireland have taken the first significant step towards achieving their own right to choose.'

The Contents

The Report which follows contains eight chapters.

1. Chapter 1, the current chapter, is introductory, and considers the reasons for the International Tribunal on Abortion. It lists the panel members and the groups which submitted evidence. Finally, it seeks to consider whether or not the International Tribunal was a success.

2. Chapter 2 looks at some of the milestones in the campaign to extend the 1967 Abortion Act to Northern Ireland. It does so through summaries of the evidence of the first Northern Ireland Abortion Law Reform Association, which existed in the early 1970s, the Northern Ireland Abortion Campaign, and the current Northern Ireland Abortion Law Reform Association. It also gives a sense of the social climate in which such campaigning groups have to operate by presenting the findings of a NIALRA survey of the opinions of political parties in Northern Ireland, a NIALRA

survey of the opinions of health professionals on the extension of the 1967 Act, and a detailed summary of the debate at the Northern Ireland Assembly in February 1984, when 21 of Northern Ireland's MPs discussed the issue of abortion.

3. Chapter 3 summarises the evidence given to the Tribunal by referral and support groups, in particular, the Ulster Pregnancy Advisory Association, the Family Planning Association, Liverpool Abortion Support Services, the Irish Women's Abortion Support Group, the Union of Students in Ireland, the British Pregnancy Advisory Association and Open Line Counselling.

4. Chapter 4 summarises the evidence presented to the Tribunal by women's groups in Northern Ireland, namely, Lesbian Line, the Northern Ireland Women's Rights Movement, Rape and Incest Line, the Rape Crisis Centre and the Well Woman Centre.

5. Chapter 5 summarises some of the evidence presented in private to the Tribunal by women from Northern Ireland who have had direct experience of abortion, whether through travelling abroad, or, in one case, in Northern Ireland itself.

6. Chapter 6 considers the legal position in Northern Ireland in relation to abortion. It is mainly comprised of a summary of the evidence presented by one law lecturer who has specialised in the subject.

7. Chapter 7 considers some medical aspects of abortion in Northern Ireland, and in particular, medical consequences of the continuing exclusion of Northern Ireland from the terms of the 1967 Abortion Act. The evidence of two GPs is summarised, as well as the written evidence presented by one consultant. In addition, the personal experience of one woman at risk of giving birth to a child with spina bifida is presented.

8. Chapter 8, by way of conclusion, considers the lessons of the Tribunal and looks at some ways forward from here to the point where legal abortion is available for women from Northern Ireland **in** Northern Ireland.

Conclusion

The ultimate success would be the extension of the 1967 Abortion Act to Northern Ireland. The organisers did not believe in advance, nor do they believe afterwards, that one International Tribunal could deliver such a success. Their aims were much more limited. They were to gather together a large cross-section of people for an informed discussion of the issue.

As such, the Tribunal clearly flew in the face of current Northern Ireland Office explanations of the situation. Writing to a fellow MP who had inquired why the 1967 Abortion Act does not extend to

Northern Ireland, John Stanley, Minister of State at the Northern Ireland Office, had this to say.

'Since the introduction of direct rule in 1972 the view has been taken not to introduce a measure to change the abortion laws in the Province unless it is likely to command broad support throughout the community. Such support does not appear to exist at present.'

This letter was written on October 6, 1987. In the two days which followed the International Tribunal proved Mr. Stanley wrong. There is a large and respectable support within Northern Ireland for the extension of the 1967 Abortion Act. If the Tribunal, or this Report, convinces Northern Ireland Office policy makers of that support, then it will have done its part not only in breaking the silence but in bringing about the ending of hypocrisy whereby politicians, medics and others seem content to have Northern Ireland women obtain abortions— provided they do so somewhere else.

2.

The Campaign for Legal Abortion in Northern Ireland

Introduction

The International Tribunal on Abortion began by hearing evidence from groups which had been active on the issue of extending the 1967 Abortion Act to Northern Ireland, including the Northern Ireland Abortion Law Reform Association (NIALRA), the main organisers of the Tribunal.

Introducing the speakers, Margaret Ward, a founder member of NIALRA, pointed out the importance of remembering that the event was in fact the culmination of very many years of work by an lot of people.

> 'Other groups have gone before us and have helped to establish the route of which this Tribunal is the next stage. It is important to bear this in mind. For anyone coming new to the abortion campaign it is easy to be disillusioned. But it is important to remember that there are now people willing to come out in favour of abortion who ten years ago would not have done so. That there has been a change of climate at all is due to the hard work of people in the past. So, it is important to hear about the history of the campaign. For that reason we will start the Tribunal's proceedings with Max Goldstrom telling us about the first Northern Ireland Abortion Law Reform Association.'

The First Northern Ireland Abortion Law Reform Association

Max Goldstrom was one of the founders of the original Northern Ireland Abortion Law Reform Association, NIALRA. He recounted how the organisation had come about, as well as how its development had eventually led to the emergence of the Ulster Pregnancy Advisory Association, UPAA.

Max had arrived in Northern Ireland in 1964. Previously he had lived in Birmingham where he had been a member of the Abortion Law Reform Association, ALRA. There was no branch in Belfast, however, and only one organisation active on the question of abortion in Northern Ireland, the Belfast Humanist Association. Their campaign had next to no success. The climate within which they had to work is

13

shown by a question asked at Stormont in 1967. One MP wanted to know if the Unionist administration would extend the 1967 Act to Northern Ireland; the answer was an outright 'No'.

But during the debate at Stormont a number of MPs joked that we did not need abortion legislation here. 'We've already got it', they said, referring to the fact that, as Max Goldstrom put it, there was

> 'a sort of semi-legalised illegal abortionist who was at work in the province—a doctor who was hard up financially but was very well connected with the medical profession. He would for a fee do abortions, generally by using a syringe, and then would advise his patients to go into hospital. This was widely known. The police in fact sometimes referred people to him if they thought they were rape cases and he was also used generally by the middle classes. One or two of his patients actually died, but nothing was done about it. In fact, he would go and visit people in hospital and he was a household name for many years. In the end, he did go to jail, not for performing abortions, but for something else.'

Max Goldstrom's first active involvement on the issue of abortion came in 1969 when one of his students turned up on his doorstep late at night, pregnant and due to take her finals in about three months time. He tried to arrange an abortion for her through legitimate medical channels in Northern Ireland, only to meet with absolute rejection. Previously students from Northern Ireland used to go to Aberdeen where there was a sympathetic gynaecologist, but he was too busy to take any more women from Northern Ireland. So, Max arranged for the pregnant student to go to Birmingham where an abortion could be arranged through the British Pregnancy Advisory Service, BPAS. From that point on 'a steady trickle of people arrived at our home as the word spread that somebody knew how to refer people for abortions elsewhere'.

With a handful of colleagues Max then decided that something needed to happen in relation to abortion in Northern Ireland. The question was whether to campaign politically or to do something practical. They decided that practical involvement was more urgent; political change would be a long time coming, but meanwhile women here were continuing to have unwanted pregnancies. Out of that conclusion the Ulster Pregnancy Advisory Association formed.

Charitable status was easily obtained by submitting the identical trustees as the BPAS. But the problem then was that, being a charity, they could not campaign politically. So that was the point where, as Max put it,

> 'we decided to don a second hat and establish the Northern Ireland Abortion Law Reform Association. It was a useful organisation, but purely from the point of view of publicity. We used it as a vehicle to publicise the Ulster Pregnancy Advisory Association and the result was the UPAA flourished.'

NIALRA itself had very limited success as a campaigning organisation.

They did succeed in having one Unionist MP join on the understanding that his membership be strictly confidential! They extracted the odd concession, such as a letter from Enoch Powell admitting that Northern Ireland should be treated with parity, although he disagreed with abortion. But the campaign did not get much further than that. Eventually a number of the people involved in NIALRA left Northern Ireland altogether and the organisation dissolved.

Despite the limited success of NIALRA, Max's conclusion was far from pessimistic. UPAA has been active all the years since, and has been a lifeline to many women with unwanted pregnancies. Even at the level of campaigning the continued existence of UPAA has been important. It has meant that since 1971 there has been 'a consistent set of detailed statistics of women who went from Northern Ireland to seek abortions in England.'

The Northern Ireland Abortion Campaign

After the first NIALRA channelled its energies into the UPAA, there was a gap in campaigning for abortion. The incident which led to the next round of campaigning was the death of a young girl in Sandy Row following a backstreet abortion. It was as a result of this that a new campaign was started, a specifically feminist group with the demand of 'a woman's right to choose'. That was the Northern Ireland Abortion Campaign. The history and lessons of NIAC were presented by Marilyn Hyndman.

Marilyn recalled that her first recollection of any public discussion surrounding the issue of abortion was in the Women's Movement in Northern Ireland in the mid-1970s, particularly in the Socialist Women's Group and the Belfast Women's Collective of which she was a member. Given the taboo against even discussing the demand of the Women's Movement for the right of every woman to choose whether or not to have a safe, legal and free abortion (a taboo which has eased only slightly in the years since), it was, recounted Marilyn, virtually impossible to have an open public debate on the issue of abortion. Despite that, a highly successful conference was organised by the Belfast Women's Collective in 1979 on 'Childbirth, Contraception and Abortion', which received widespread publicity and was attended by several hundred women from all over the North of Ireland, although the emphasis by the press was placed more on childbirth than the more controversial issue of abortion.

Marilyn continued:

'The following year I met a young girl at a friend's house in Sandy Row, a working class district only a couple of streets away from where we are sitting today. A few weeks later I learnt that she was dead. She had died a horrific death from septicaemia following complications after resorting to a backstreet abortionist. Her death was the catalyst in founding the Northern Ireland Abortion Campaign, a group which believed in a woman's right to choose and was to campaign for the extension of the 1967 Abortion Act to Northern Ireland as a minimum demand. Membership was open to all women who supported these demands although the hard core of the group was made up of members of the Belfast Women's Collective, the Northern Ireland Women's Rights Movement and a representative from the Young Unionists.'

From the outset NIAC members recognised that they faced a long and hard struggle with opposition from all quarters of Northern Ireland society—the churches, the politicians, the medical profession and large numbers of Northern Ireland people.

'It was one of the few issues on which it seemed that everyone agreed, and they were all against us! To give you just one example, Frank Maguire, who was elected to Westminster on an abstentionist ticket for Fermanagh/South Tyrone as an Independent Nationalist, went to the House of Commons on two occasions, one of which was to vote for a tightening of abortion laws which did not apply in Northern Ireland anyway.'

NIAC therefore judged that their task was to bring the issue out into the open, to break the silence. To this end they produced leaflets which were given out every Saturday in Cornmarket and sparked off conversations and debates with shoppers and passers-by. They put up posters all over town, held press and television interviews, produced a pamphlet, *A Woman's Choice: The case for free, legal and safe abortion in Northern Ireland,* and organised an abortion conference in Belfast.

October 1981 proved to be a high point in the campaign, when Marilyn and another member of NIAC travelled to London to deliver over 600 coat hangers and imitation travel tickets to each Member of Parliament. This was to symbolise the two ways in which women from Northern Ireland could obtain an abortion—the backstreet or a journey to England for a termination in a private clinic. The story was reported in national newspapers both in Ireland and Britain, with the main newspaper in Northern Ireland, the *Belfast Telegraph* , coming out in support of the demand to extend the 1967 Abortion Act to the North. Later several trade unions came out in active support of the demand, most notably the National Union of Public Employees, and in 1985 the British Medical Association adopted the following motion as their policy by a substantial majority:

'This meeting urges the BMA to actively pursue its policy of support for the extension of the 1967 Abortion Act to Northern Ireland'.

Marilyn went on to say that, while NIAC recognised the political sensitivity of extending a British law to Northern Ireland to certain sections of Northern Ireland society, the organisation felt that it was a practical demand which stood a reasonable chance of success. They were also aware that in common with other parts of the United Kingdom, most notably the Birmingham area, the extension of the Act might not in itself ensure that women in Northern would be adequately catered for by the National Health Service as regards abortion; but extension would allow private non-profit distributing clinics to be set up. Also, women in the South would then only be a train journey away from facilities and support services. Such an arrangement would be far from perfect but would still be an improvement on the present situation where it can, for example, be less expensive for women to travel from Spain for an abortion in London than from the South of Ireland.

One other success chalked up by NIAC was recounted by Marilyn. In April 1982, they decided to gauge one section of Northern Ireland opinion by carrying out a survey of General Practitioners, as they are often the first people to whom women will go when they wish a pregnancy confirmed. The survey showed that a sizeable number of GPs were in favour of a reform of the law (57%), that 14.8% suspected that their patients had attempted to procure a miscarriage and that 79.9% informed their patients about abortion facilities in England. GPs were most concerned about the psychological effects upon women who were forced to travel to England and the lack of any medical support en route. 14% were against abortion under any circumstances.

Marilyn concluded that

> 'the results of this survey showed that abortion is an issue in Northern Ireland, that unwanted pregnancies do occur and that the only choices open to women with unwanted pregnancies are either the dangers of a backstreet abortion, risking sterility and death, or an expensive trip to England.'

Finally, in 1984 NIAC was instrumental in the formation of a sister organisation, the Northern Ireland Abortion Law Reform Association, with a single demand, the extension of the 1967 Abortion Act to Northern Ireland. It was decided that membership would be open to both men and women who supported this demand.

It was from this new organisation, NIALRA, that the conference next heard evidence. Anna Eggert told the story of the second organisation to bear the name NIALRA.

The Northern Ireland Abortion Law Reform Association (Number Two)

Anna began by explaining why NIAC felt it necessary to have NIALRA as a sister organisation. There were two main reasons. Firstly, NIAC felt that it could not really get any further, and wanted to open up the campaign. NIAC had done everything they could to raise the issue of abortion. In a society as repressive as ours, said Anna, this surely is not easy. To get any further at all it seemed more practicable to leave the 'women's right to choose' position and open up a single issue campaign, which is what was done. It was decided to have a single demand, the extension of the 1967 Abortion Act, and membership would then be open to anyone, male or female, who agreed with this one demand. As a result, NIALRA became quite a mixed group with members of different political affiliations, religious or moral beliefs and, of course, both genders. Anna stressed that this was a deliberate policy in the foundation of NIALRA.

'Unfortunately at least in our society, a women-only group is still likely to be seen as a group of "raving feminists", but for the campaign we wanted to launch we needed a more "respectable image" than that.'

She went on to say that NIALRA is, comparatively speaking, a small group. However, it has a core of committed and active members— committed, because they know of the need for the campaign, because they know of the hardship and suffering that women here have to go through, and because they know that a lot of this is additional burden, unnecessary if only the law was changed.

There was one thing which, Anna pointed out, needed to be made perfectly clear.

'We are not "Pro-Abortionists" in the way that anti-abortion campaigners like to portray us; we do not believe that abortion always is the one and only way out, and we certainly don't force any woman to have an abortion. But history has shown that abortions take place, no matter what the law. We want those sad cases in which abortion is the only way out to be legal, to be safe and to be free.'

'We believe that a woman faced with an unwanted, difficult, physically or mentally problematic pregnancy, a woman in social, personal, financial or whatever difficulties, should have the right to counselling, the right to get any relevant information and the right to get the appropriate services, and this includes the provision of legal abortions.'

Without wishing to preempt the session on the legal situation to occur the next day, Anna felt that it was extremely important to devote some time at this introductory session to considering the law. The law governing abortion in Northern Ireland, she argued, is both outdated and ambiguous. Basically abortion is covered by a piece of Victorian legislation, the 1861 *Offences Against the Person Act* , which, among many other issues, totally forbids abortion, under threat of penal servitude for up to life. In 1945 the *Infant Life (Preservation) Act* , which had been introduced in Britain in 1929, was extended to Northern Ireland. As the title suggests, it mainly concerns itself with preservation of infant life and was a measure to try and cut down high rates of infanticide. It is only in this context that it is possible to understand why, in order to save the life of the woman, this Act allows abortions only after 28 weeks of duration. So, the ludicrous situation in Northern Ireland is that it is legally possible to terminate a pregnancy when this is already very advanced while at the same time, because of the absence of the 1967 Abortion Act, being unable to perform abortions legally on many women at much earlier stages of pregnancy.

NIALRA's conclusion is clear:

'Owing to the confusion over the law, doctors are not free to act in the best interest of their patients. Women in Northern Ireland are denied medical facilities, they are denied the benefits of tried and tested medical advances in ante-natal screening due to the absence of routine and easily available facilities for the termination of abnormal pregnancies.'

Anna finally mentioned another reason for NIALRA's concern about the current legal situation, namely that the law as it stands discriminates against working class and poor women who cannot find the money to go to Britain and pay for an abortion.

In concluding, Anna stated:

'The situation we are in raises a lot of questions; the answers—the abortions needed for women here—get exported. Since the introduction of the Abortion Act in Britain, more than 20,000 women from Northern Ireland have travelled to England for an abortion. Local politicians and church leaders don't want to hear about it, refuse to recognize the problem. In fact, many of our representatives, whether in politics, the churches or trade unions, are happy the way things are. Everybody knows what is going on but nobody wants to tackle the issue. Again this reflects the kind of society we live in, if people who know about the problems, possibly even are involved in the "abortion tourism", don't dare to come and speak about it because anti-abortionists will label them.'

Like NIAC and the first NIALRA before it, NIALRA has, since its beginning in February 1984, tried to break the silence about abortion in Northern Ireland. Initially they produced a leaflet stating the situation and calling for change in the law. In the summer of 1985 this was followed by the publication of a more comprehensive pamphlet. Every opportunity was taken to speak in schools, universities and colleges, and to publicise the demand for the extension of the 1967 Abortion Act at conferences and through the media.

Members of NIALRA felt that the twentieth anniversary of the passing of the 1967 Act in Britain presented the opportunity for a major event to raise the issue and break the silence around a very old dilemma. Out of that belief came the International Tribunal on Abortion. Contacts were made with women's groups, the voluntary sector and the medical and legal professions in the task of assembling evidence for the Tribunal. In addition, every local political party was asked for its position on the issue of abortion, and a questionnaire was sent to doctors and other relevant professionals on the issue of the extension of the 1967 Abortion Act to Northern Ireland. Iris Adare presented the results of the survey of political parties, and Bill Rolston the results of the questionnaire.

Together these two surveys give a clear picture of the general anti-abortion atmosphere in which NIALRA has had to operate.

19

NIALRA's Survey of Political Parties

Iris Adare began by telling the audience that, in pursuance of their aim of putting together evidence and experiences from a wide range of concerned groups and individuals, the organising committee of the International Tribunal on Abortion felt that it would be useful, and indeed necessary, to clarify the current position of organised political groupings in Northern Ireland on this issue.

Initially a statement was sought from each party/grouping regarding the extension of the Abortion Act 1967 to Northern Ireland. A total of twelve were written to, of whom eight replied. Of these eight, there were six who did not offer full support: three were totally opposed, while the other three have no party policy on the matter, leaving it as an 'issue of conscience' for individuals to decide for themselves. Only one offered full support, with a second being the representative of a party which does not organise here and therefore expressing the opinion of local members only.

Those who did not support the extension of the Act to Northern Ireland were then sent a second letter asking what measures, if any, their party would take to help a woman coming to their advice centres with this problem, and/or what measures they would be prepared to support in coping with this issue. Iris then presented a brief resume of these exchanges.

The Ulster Unionist Party has no 'party' attitude, as a free vote system was said to apply on issues of conscience. The Party stated that Ulster Unionist MPs would probably oppose the extension of the Act. It was agreed that some reform was needed, but not to the point of supporting extension.

The Popular Unionist Party made no direct comment. The request was handed over to a woman representative. There was no reply to a second letter.

The Democratic Unionist Party does not support extension. No reply to a second letter was received.

The Social Democratic and Labour Party's position is one of strong opposition to extension. It was stated that John Hume (the Party leader) personally opposes the move very strongly. The Party prefers to support 'caring' groups helping with the problems which force women to seek abortions. As regards therapeutic abortions, the Party does not accept abortion as therapy.

The Alliance Party has no party policy. It is an issue of conscience left to individuals. The request for information was passed to Ms. N. McIntyre. A second letter was sent to party spokesperson Fionnuala Cook. No reply was received.

The Workers' Party did not reply.

Sinn Féin referred to their statement of policy (of the 1986 Ard Fheis): the Party opposes those forces in society which 'cause women to seek abortions'; it opposes abortion 'as a means of birth control', but accepts the need for abortion where life is at risk, *etc.* The Party was contacted for an interview, but replied that everyone was too busy (it was an election period); they said they would be back in contact afterwards, but were not. No reply was received to a second letter.

The Progressive Unionist Party did not reply.

The Communist Party stated its full support for the extension of the 1967 Act.

The Social Democratic Party does not organise in Northern Ireland, but the local representative supports extension and feels that most local members would also. He said he would contact to arrange a meeting, but did not.

People's Democracy did not reply.

Labour Party '87 did not reply.

Having presented the above results, Iris concluded with the following statement:

> 'These attitudes call into question what role political parties actually fulfill in issues such as these *vis-a-vis* the voting public; which is dog and which tail, and who wags who? Do these policies fairly reflect the views of the electorate, or only the views of the politicians as individuals, or what the parties perceive to be the views of the people? Can a party leave such issues to the "individual consciences" of its members and then claim to be representatives of the people and the people's wishes? Is it really a way of avoiding an issue seen as too controversial, or in fact an issue largely concerned "only with women's affairs" and therefore deemed to be of secondary, marginal importance? Who is representing the views of the 20,957 women who travelled from Northern Ireland to England in the past twenty years? In the absence of an objective referendum, it is very difficult to discern what process is used to determine public opinion.'

NIALRA's Survey of Health Professionals and Advice Workers

Bill Rolston began by pointing out that in 1985 NIALRA, in the knowledge that no MP from Northern Ireland was willing to introduce a Private Member's Bill in Westminster to extend the 1967 Abortion Act to Northern Ireland, approached a number of potentially sympathetic MPs in Britain asking them to consider introducing such a bill. In the event, even the most sympathetic MPs felt that there were any number of causes closer to home to command their attention. However, a spin-off of this attempt is that one MP, Ken Weetch, wrote to the Northern Ireland Office on NIALRA's behalf asking why the 1967 Act did not extend to Northern Ireland.

Northern Ireland Office Minister Nicholas Scott replied:

> 'Since the introduction of direct rule in 1972 the view has been taken not to introduce a measure to change the abortion laws in Northern Ireland unless it is likely to command broad support among the people of the Province. Such support does not appear to exist at present. Last year the Northern Ireland Assembly resolved to oppose the extension of the 1967 Act to the Province

and 14 of the 26 District and Borough Councils were reported to have done likewise. Subsequent press articles suggested that the Protestant and Roman Catholic Churches and some Northern Ireland MPs still hold strong views against abortion.'

By way of reply to this statement, Bill said that it is NIALRA's position that the decisions of over 20,000 women from Northern Ireland—women from the whole range of class positions and political identities—to travel to Britain for abortions in the last twenty years represents a proven, substantial and thoroughly respectable demand for the availability of abortion facilities here at home. But in an attempt to back up this sentiment with some survey material, NIALRA, in preparation for the International Tribunal on Abortion, sent out just over 1,000 questionnaires to as large a sample as possible of doctors, district and community nurses and midwives, health visitors, senior and principal social workers with responsibility for childcare, student counsellors, and consultant obstetricians, gynaecologists and psychiatrists.

Only 201 completed questionnaires were returned, a response rate of just about 20%. In a situation where the organisation doing the postal survey is not only unknown to most of those surveyed but also where the topic being researched is one around which there is such a taboo to open and rational discussion, the response was judged to be as good as could be expected.

As for the actual results of the questionnaire, the following facts emerged: 64% of those who replied were doctors or consultants, 22% were community or district nurses, midwives or health visitors, 9% were people who worked in an advice capacity with women, whether as social workers, advice workers, *etc.*,and 4% gave no occupation at all.

The respondents were asked if they favoured the extension of the 1967 Abortion Act to Northern Ireland. 54.3% said they were in favour, 42.7% were against and 2.7% were uncommitted. A more interesting picture emerged when this was broken down further. 58.1% of doctors and consultants were in favour of the extension, 39.5% were against and 2.3% uncommitted.

As regards community or district nurses, midwives and health visitors, 35.5% were in favour of extension, while 60% were opposed; 4.4% were uncommitted.

Finally, in relation to advice workers, 84.2% were in favour of extension, 5.3% opposed, and 10.5% uncommitted.

Bill felt that two points were worth drawing attention to in the above. Firstly, the figure for doctors and consultants in favour of the extension of the 1967 Act was remarkably close to that produced by NIAC (in their 1982 survey) for doctors in favour of legislation to make abortion easier: 58% for NIALRA in 1987, compared to 57% for NIAC five years earlier. Secondly, there were stark differences in the answers to this question as regards different professional groups; the advice workers were by far most in favour, with a small majority of doctors and consultants in favour, while community and district nurses, midwives and health visitors were quite definitively against.

Respondents were also asked to say whether they would still be in favour of the extension of the 1967 Act if public opinion here was opposed to such extension; of those who were in favour of extension, 82% said they would continue to be in favour even if public opinion was against such extension; 12.6% were opposed, and 4.5% were unsure.

Finally, the data were examined to see if there was any correlation between whether those who replied had any contact with women seeking help on abortion and their position on the extension of the 1967 Act. A stark result emerged: 61.3% of those who had any contact at all with women seeking help on abortion were in favour of the extension, with 34.7% not in favour of extension and 4.2% undecided. On the other hand, a staggering 78.6% of those who had no contact with women seeking help on abortion were opposed to the extension of the 1967 Act, while only 17.8% were in favour; 3.6% were undecided. Bill concluded:

> 'It is quite clear that those who have direct professional contact with women who want abortions are very likely to recognise the need for abortion facilities here, while those most vehemently opposed to abortion facilities here are so from a position of total professional ignorance.'

Space was left on the questionnaire for people to add any comments.

Bill reported that imposing moral values was at the forefront of the arguments for not extending the 1967 Act. 'Perhaps there are doctors in Northern Ireland prepared to commit murder at a price', said one doctor, but she or he was not one of them. The word 'murder', often heavily underlined, was quite frequent in these replies. Slightly more sophisticated was the argument of one health visitor that non-violence to the unborn spills over into non-violence to living children, and conversely violence to the unborn has its counterpart in violence to living children; but no evidence was provided as to whether there was much less violence against children here than in countries where abortion was widely available.

Abortion was said to be against God's law. At one remove from this was the argument that abortion should not be available because it was abhorrent to the religious convictions of the vast majority of people in Northern Ireland.

Beyond the moral arguments, some more pragmatic reasons were put forward for non-extension. Mental trauma follows on abortion, stated one midwife. For some this trauma seems to begin even prior to abortion. A district nurse: 'I feel the exclusion should continue as women would only be faced with a further dilemma if abortion was freely available, at a time when they are unable to make a rational decision.' So, the decision—a negative one—must be made for them by others. Perhaps this is the same argument as that made by one doctor, that if the option is not available, then people won't ask for it!

Having abortion available here would put an unnecessary strain on the health service, said one GP, especially with the big influx of 'girls from the Republic'. A family planning doctor stressed that we live in a small country and that having to travel to Britain guaranteed confidentiality. But perhaps saddest of all was the consultant surgeon who said that, while he personally was in favour of abortion, there was no point having a head-on clash with anti-abortionists on the issue; travel to Britain was the easy option. This, said Bill, is precisely the 'conspiracy of silence' NIALRA is trying to break.

An easy option of a different kind was stressed by a number of people. One GP was of the opinion that women only wanted terminations because it was inconvenient for them to be pregnant; the very adjective chosen here conveys a sense of selfishness on the part of the women. Another doctor was more explicit; abortion is an easy solution to a problem caused by this permissive age and only encourages more permissiveness. And a district nursing sister stated that abortion is the easy way out of a situation which should never have happened in the first place; people should learn 'more discipline in relation to desires', she added.

Turning then to the replies of those in favour of the extension, Bill reported that a few respondents stressed the fact that continuing with an unwanted pregnancy, especially when the mother was a quite young single parent, could lead to neglect and abuse; as one social worker put it, 'unwanted children continue to pay the price'. But a much more common reason for supporting the extension was that the absence of the Act is discriminatory. As one doctor said, we pay the same taxes here, so why don't we have the same rights? Also stressed was the notion that present policy is in effect discrimination against poorer women: as one consultant gynaecologist put it, it increases the under-privilege of already underprivileged women.

By far the most mentioned aspect was the physical and emotional burden of having to travel to Britain to have an abortion. One health visitor pointed out that an already traumatic experience is made worse by having to travel alone to a strange place. A doctor stressed the physical hardship of travel, especially back from Britain soon after an operation. Medical reasons also came to the fore in other replies. One family planning doctor stressed that the absence of abortion facilities locally encouraged dangerous attempts at 'self-termination'. Another doctor pointed out that often even highly necessary abortions were not performed here because of legal ambiguity. One other doctor stressed that this legal ambiguity allowed doctors here to opt out of taking a stand on what was a crucial aspect of patient care.

The hypocrisy of our current arrangements thus was central in a number of replies. One consultant replied: 'most anti-abortion fanatics have a complete change when their own relatives are involved, regardless of religious persuasion. The hypocrisy has to be seen to be believed.' A GP made a similar point: 'I have arranged abortions for members of families who publicly oppose abortion vociferously. It is easy to adopt a righteous stance if not directly affected.' From a consideration of hypocrisy it is a short step to the conclusion of one doctor that it is wrong to impose one's own moral values on others.

In conclusion, Bill stated:

'To return to our overall figure for support for extension of the 1967 Act: 58.1% may not be appear to be a very high level of support. But it is worth pointing out that it is a higher percentage than that which elected many of the politicians, churchmen and others who work against the provision of legal abortion in Northern Ireland.'

The Assembly Debate on Abortion, 1984

A final measure of the social climate within which the campaign for the extension of the 1967 Abortion Act has to operate was presented as written evidence to the Tribunal. It was a full account of the debate in the Northern Ireland Assembly on February 29, 1984, when the issue of abortion was discussed. The summary of that debate which follows confirms the findings of NIALRA in its survey of political parties, presented above.

The motion debated was as follows: 'That this Assembly opposes the extension of the Abortion Act 1967, or any like legislation, to Northern Ireland.' Twenty one Members were present, representing the Democratic Unionist and the Alliance Parties. For political reasons the elected representatives of the Official Unionist Party were not present, and those of the Social Democratic and Labour Party and Sinn Fein had not taken their seats in the Assembly.

The motion was moved by the Rev. Ivan Foster, who defined the issue of abortion as 'the termination of the life of an unborn child ... the unlawful killing of children'. His general moral viewpoint found expression in the claim that 'the family is the very hub of humanity; it is the central unit of all properly ordered societies ... The fall of any great nation or any great empire had as its root cause the breaking down of family morality.' In turn, this morality had its foundation in Christianity, and Ivan Foster quoted liberally from the Scriptures: the words of the Psalms, Jeremiah the Prophet, and the angel who addressed Zacharias. He cited a verse of Scripture which 'prophesies a time when men will put lightness for darkness and darkness for light.' Nothing, he continued,

'demonstrates more clearly that that terrible age is indeed dawning upon us, than the extermination of two million unborn children in the name of humanity and in the name of medical advancement and in the name of enhancing the lives of our citizens.'

Ivan Foster admitted that 'I am much more at ease with the Bible in my hand and my finger waving in the air than perhaps I am with an Order Paper.' Aside from the Scriptures, he relied in his arguments against legal abortion upon studies from 1972 and 1975. These, he alleged, proved that the 1967 Abortion Act had not eliminated illegal abortions, that 'women who have an abortion tend to be more suicidal than most', that abortion 'increases the risk of a woman giving birth to a handicapped child ... owing to damage to the womb', and that women who have had abortions are much more likely to miscarry during any subsequent pregancy.

Pro-abortionists, he said, claimed that 'if there is abortion, then that will do away with unwanted children.' They also claimed that abortion 'will remove the burden of a handicapped child.' In this, their claim was akin to Adolf Hitler's, but

> 'Adolf Hitler had more charity in him than the abortionists because the abortionists would seek to put to death a child with no defects.'

Ivan Foster referred to 'a sizeable pro-abortionist lobby' in Northern Ireland. However, they were 'aided by an influx of abortionists from Southern Ireland who, finding themselves unable to take their campaign any further because of their constitution, are coming up here to turn Northern Ireland into an abortionists' haven.' The existence of such a lobby was, in a society 'plagued by terrorism', 'incredible'. Equally incredible was the fact that within newspapers which 'use the harshest terms to describe those who gun down innocent people' were 'the words of those who advocate the killing of children'.

As the solitary opponent of the motion, Mr. Addie Morrow recognised the strong and sincere convictions of those who opposed abortion. He did not believe that those who wanted the 1967 Act extended could rightly be depicted as 'going out onto the street looking for people and trying to get them to have abortions'. He argued that 'it is impossible for a mere man to really understand how a woman would feel about an unwanted pregnancy' and regretted that debates on abortion 'very often take place when no women are present', such that 'the sex most affected by this is not able to contribute'. He maintained that the legal position concerning abortion in Northern Ireland was 'very obscure', but that it had 'certainly not prevented women from getting abortions'. However, money was necessary to travel to Britain for a legal abortion and 'it does not seem to be very fair when there is a law for the rich and another for the poor'.

Mr. Morrow wondered if there was any point to a test for spina bifida if 'in effect, we are not going to do anything about its results.' He also pointed out that several contraceptive methods 'used quite openly ... in this country at the minute' were strictly, and within the terms of the anti-abortionist arguments, abortions. Pressed to say whether abortion was not the taking of life, Mr. Morrow said: 'A mother and an unborn child presents a unique situation. It is something which cannot be confused with murder outside the womb. That is emotive language.' He referred to the situation in which a woman is raped and asked the other Members: 'If this happened to one's own daughter of, say 14 years or 15 years, just how would one carry the argument through?'

Mr. Morrow said that he might be more swayed by the arguments for the motion if we were living in a caring society, 'but we are not a caring society'. He referred to 'the terrible tragedy of that young girl in the South of Ireland who died at the back of a hedge', and to the young girl in Belfast who left school to have her baby:

> 'When she went back she was rejected and told that there was no place for her there. While society acts in this unchristian, inhuman way I do not believe it has the right to force its hypocritical morals down the throats of these unfortunate women.'

Mr. William Thomson, speaking 'as a Methodist', opposed the motion. He could see no other definition for abortion than 'murder', and said that the numbers of abortions taking place in Britain were 'staggering'.

> 'It is a disgrace, in this so-called Christian country, that this is allowed to go on. This is an indication that we are no longer a Christian country, rather we are a heathen country because we allow this butchery and murder to continue unabated.'

Mr. Thomson stated his belief to be that 'the Bible is man's rule and guide and what is contained in the Scriptures ought to be our guide in life.' Those Scriptures taught that any sexual relationships outside marriage 'are contrary to the Word of God, are sinful and will be judged by Almighty God.' The highest proportion of abortions were, he said, carried out on unmarried girls between the ages of 16 and 24: 'These girls have had sexual relationships outside marriage; they have been committing fornication and have had to have abortions to get rid of the resulting problems'. Indeed most abortions, he said, 'are as a result of fornication and lust and not of conception within marriage.'

Challenged by Mr. Morrow as to whether he did not think unwanted pregnancies amongst young girls were a result of ignorance and a lack of sex education, Mr. Thomson replied:

> 'I think we have more sex education today than we ever had before, and I do not believe that the girls who get pregnant are innocent. It may be that some are innocent, because their parents have not warned them or brought them up properly, told them the facts of life and taught them the Scriptures. I do believe that in the breast of every woman there is knowledge of what is right and what is wrong and knowledge that to act in this fashion is wrong.'

The number of abortions being carried out today, he continued, illustrated 'the ungodliness of our nation, the depravity of our age and how men and women have forgotten the things of God.' 'When you reject the things of God', he said, 'the things of the Devil come to the forefront.'

The results of abortion on women were, he alleged, 'severe': '10 per cent of women who have had an abortion will never bear children again because they have become barren as a result', and of the remainder '17.5 per cent of them will miscarry'. On the question of rape, Mr. Thomson stated, 'The truth is that only a very, very small percentage of girls who are raped become pregnant.' Challenged as to his view on abortifacient contraceptives, Mr. Thomson said: 'I am not an authority on contraception', but that if they worked in the way claimed, he could not agree with them. Returning to the subject of rape, he said that the circumstances were not any different from those where a woman has been knocked down by a drunken driver, and has to bear the subsequent physical and psychological damage:

> 'The truth of the matter is that there are many tragedies in life which cannot be remedied and we have to accept them, and I think that rape, in this situation, must come under one of those.'

Similarly

> 'we have to leave the question of deformity in the providence of Almighty God and, if a child is conceived in love, then I think that the parents ought to be quite willing to accept what God has ordained should be born to them ... Even if a deformed child is born after rape it ought to be accepted as the will of God.'

The Rev. Ivan Foster interrupted to state that abortion in the case of rape constituted a 'very perverted form of fairness', since 'we should destroy the only innocent party in that tragic affair, namely the child conceived.'

Mr. Thomson continued by stating that 'when one moves away from scriptural truth and principles laid down in Scripture one enters into a realm where there is perverted reasoning and perverted actions.' The pro-abortionists were wrong to argue that a woman had a right to choose whether or not to keep the baby: 'The woman has already exercised her choice when she became pregnant. That is the time of choice; whether to become pregant or not.' If unwanted pregnancies occurred within marriage then 'that is not the right marriage; it is the wrong concept of marriage because, within a true marriage, there should not be children like that.' He later continued,

> 'I do not believe that it is possible from a scriptural point of view to conceive a child in love outside of marriage, and similarly in an ideal situation, children ought not to be conceived within marriage if the parents do not love each other and do not wish that child to be born. Anything outside that ideal is wrong and sinful.'.

Mr. Seamus Close referred to those who fought for the right of abortion as 'either misguided or ... total hypocrites ... They spew their murderous arguments.' Those doctors who defended such a right were 'a disgrace to their profession'. Abortion, he said, rested 'on the extremely dangerous principle that the small and weak are inferior, and that some human beings are disposable.' Though he did not believe in capital punishment, 'those who kill, be it the unborn child or anyone else, should be amenable to the law that exists at that particular time.' He compared pro-abortionists to terrorists in seeking to supply reasons for 'their barbarous acts' and 'their butchery'. 'All organised wrong-doing generates its own verbal gymnastics in an attempt to disguise its actions.'

Mr. Seawright also used the analogy of terrorism:

> 'as we abhor the slaughter and maiming of individuals outside the

womb through terrorism, we politicians, if we are to be consistent, must, by the same force of argument and by the same resolve, condemn the slaughter of innocent individuals inside the womb.'

Returning to the hypothetical case in which his own daughter might become pregnant through rape, Mr. Seawright said,

> 'while it would be something of a catastrophe if that happened to my daughter, I would like to think that while my daughter would have to live with that catastrophe she would accept that even though her child was fathered by a brutal, terrible rapist—who I believe should be put to death as I believe in capital punishment for rapists, and I make no apology for that, although I cannot justify the taking of the life of a totally and absolutely innocent party—the baby was innocent and was entitled to live and should be cherished.'

Mr. Gordon Mawhinney stated that, 'in view of the ignorance of some honourable Members about the method of operation' of the IUD and day-after pill, it was worth adding that this ignorance was shared by many women using these contraceptive devices. He knew of one girl who was using an IUD and who did not know that 'she was in fact aborting her pregnancy each time.' He had taken the opportunity to watch a film of an abortion. He 'was distressed, not only at the horrific sight of seeing another human being ripped apart by a vacuum pump, but by the detached operation of the staff who performed the operation.' Such detachment was 'remarkable' and 'a sad reflection on our society that highly skilled people trained at public expense should use those skills in the destruction of human life.' Many of those who performed abortions

> 'do so with a single motive—money. Abortion is big business. There is a lot of money in abortion, and a lot of doctors use the skills acquired at public expense for private gain.'

Mr. Wesley Pentland asked whether Mr. Mawhinney would agree

> 'that the Almighty Creator provided within woman a mechanism whereby, if either she as the mother had some inherent fault or the child had some fault, what is known as miscarriage—that very distressing situation—or a woman's own abortion, and that therefore a greater mind has been brought to bear upon whether abortion should take place or not and that, after that, if conception is allowed to proceed, then it is in the plan of a mighty and sovereign Creator.'

Winding up the debate, the Rev. Ivan Foster referred to the 'rather lonely crusade' of Mr. Morrow, whom he compared to a 'Daniel' or a 'Nebuchadnezzar'. He welcomed the support given to the motion and noted that

> 'Jews, gentiles and atheists have been mentioned. I welcome support for this motion ... from whatever source it comes. Whoever welcomes this principle is, of course, espousing a biblical principle.'

Concluding, he said that

> 'I am glad that there is on record the strong feelings that have been voiced in opposition to abortion, and I trust that this country will be saved, with all its troubles and with all its blood-stained history, from an even greater stain and an even greater crime: the crime and the stain of the blood of innocent children.'

When the Assembly divided, there were 20 in favour of the motion and 1 opposing it.

3.

Referral and Support Groups

The Tribunal heard evidence presented by a number of referral groups in both the North and South of Ireland who provide non-directive counselling to pregnant women. Their evidence was confined to what information they could provide about Irish women going to Britain for abortions.

In addition, evidence was presented by a number of support groups in Britain and the Irish Republic.

The Ulster Pregnancy Advisory Association and the Family Planning Association

The Ulster Pregnancy Advisory Association (UPAA) and the Family Planning Association (FPA) gave evidence to the Tribunal based on their work as counselling and referral agencies in Northern Ireland. Both organisations spoke of the unnecessary pain and trauma caused by the lonely and difficult journey to England for an abortion.

The UPAA was established in 1970 after the attempted suicide of an nineteen year old girl who, on finding that she was pregnant and unable to procure an abortion locally, had jumped into the River Lagan.

Seventeen years later the UPAA are answering calls daily from women who feel as desperate, isolated and rejected as that girl. The UPAA considered that a great deal of the fault lies in the lack of adequate sex education in schools and in the home and that more could be done by both parents and teachers to ensure that young people are provided with reliable information with which to make responsible decisions.

About 50% of the women coming to the UPAA are referred by a doctor. The other 50% is made up of referrals from social workers, probation officers, family planning clinics, the Samaritans, health visitors and Citizens Advice Bureaux, as well as women who refer themselves. The UPAA advertises nightly in the *Belfast Telegraph* .

The FPA's experience in this area of referral has been one of many distressed women desperately trying to find the right agency for help. The FPA considers that much more could be done by doctors, pregnancy testing agencies and health clinics in providing a choice of guidance to pregnant women who want to know more about the alternatives available. This, they felt, would ensure that women do not arrive in a distressed and confused state, weighed down by the 'bad treatment they have received from the "caring professionals" and "caring volunteers"'.

Both organisations offer women a pregnancy test. The FPA found that many women, especially young women and girls, delay having a pregnancy test until their second period is missed—which means that they could be anything up to 12-13 weeks pregnant before they finally accept that they must seek some information and help.

Women seeking help and advice are first asked what kind of information they require. The UPAA has nine women counsellors, eight of whom work from their own homes, so that women can be seen in a warm and caring non-institutional atmosphere. The UPAA also offer a service two evenings a week from their headquarters to women who are unable to avail of their daytime service. Women seeking help may come alone to an appointment or be accompanied by a person of their own choice. Common worries and fears concern the reactions of families, parents and partners. Women need a great deal of time to work out these relationships before they can start expressing their own feelings. The FPA found that a lot of women at a first appointment want to rush from a positive pregnancy test to an abortion and that there was a need to help them slow down and accept the situation and explore their problems and emotions. Both organisations consider it imperative that every woman is counselled and asked to look at all her options—if she feels she cannot consider continuing with the pregnancy/fostering/adoption, an abortion referral is made under the 1967 Abortion Act. Both organisations explain exactly what is going to happen to the women if they choose to go to England for an abortion, what to bring with them, how much the operation costs, where they are going to stay, *etc.*, in an effort to instil as much confidence as is possible before they set off on their journey.

Joan Wilson of the UPAA acknowledged that

'in very exceptional cases, and I mean very exceptional, a woman may get an abortion here in Northern Ireland. Very often it means a long wait and with no guarantee that at the end anyone is going to say yes. We have women who have been raped, we have menopausal women who have thought that they were quite safe—they weren't going to become pregnant again—turned down.'

So the majority of women have to travel to England. In 1986 the UPAA arranged 1,190 abortions and up until the end of August 1987 (the year of the International Tribunal on Abortion) the total was 800. Women from Northern Ireland must pay for an abortion in England, upwards of £200.

The FPA found that many women do not have that kind of money available to them and that the fear of having to confide in another person to ask for the money was often expressed, especially by younger women.

'Many young people are sent away from agencies to try to find the money to finance their travel and accommodation. Some are

32

forced to tell their parents or boyfriends; some just don't return and there is no way to follow up or find out what happens to them.'

Both organisations commented on the marked increase in Northern Ireland women travelling to England for abortions over the past twenty years and the great need for abortion to be available in Northern Ireland. The FPA commented that

'many women are shocked and fears and feelings of isolation increase when, having made the decision to terminate their pregnancy or to find out more information on termination, they discover that they are involved in an action that is totally opposed by the society in which they live. This effects not only their emotional feelings of isolation but also physical care both before and after the operation. Many women, because of financial constraints, travel alone on the overnight ferry and arrive in a strange town, tired, frightened, confused (about how to get to the clinic) and very lonely.'

The UPAA runs an after-care clinic at their premises on the Lisburn Road. This is seen as a very important part of their service in that a check-up must be done 4 to 6 weeks after an abortion; it also gives an opportunity for women to talk to a woman doctor about their experience. The doctor is also a family planning expert. The FPA also considers that after-care is very important and that

'many women express concern over where they should go for a check-up when they come back home. They fear other people's attitudes and values and worry about going for information on contraception in case somebody finds out about the abortion.'

The FPA encourages women to return to them any time after they return home to talk over anything they feel unsure about.

The FPA also highlighted the specific problems of single mothers who have

'the added difficulty of finding someone to look after their children while they are out of the country. Many worry about the children receiving proper care in their absence and have the added emotional stress of missing their children. It also means that they may have to confide in people they may not otherwise have told. Working women also express concern over getting time off work and usually try and arrange their operation over the weekend. This means they travel on the overnight ferry on Friday night, have the operation on Saturday and return on the Sunday night ferry in time for work on Monday.'

The FPA will refer women to the UPAA or, if the women choose, to the BPAS (British Pregnancy Advisory Service) directly. In the case of women living too far away from Belfast to come into the office, as much work as possible is done over the phone, giving the woman a choice of seeing a UPAA counsellor in her area or making her own arrangements.

The UPAA concluded its evidence to the Tribunal by stating that 'in face of the extreme opposition to abortion being made available to Northern Irish women, we, in the UPAA, go about our work quietly and competently offering women a caring, confidential service, women who might otherwise be abandoned. All of us here today know deep down in our hearts that any woman intent upon having an abortion where there isn't one safely and legally available will resort to the backstreet abortionists and all that that involves. It has always been like that and it always will be like that. Let us hope that some sense will prevail in Northern Ireland and that its citizens will come to recognise that they have a responsibility to guarantee every women the freedom of reproductive choice.'

Box 3.1

Common Worries and Fears of Women Seeking an Abortion

Compiled for the Tribunal by the FPA

Travelling alone and getting lost.
Being alone overnight.
What will the clinic be like?
Will it hurt?
What will it feel like?
Will anybody be able to tell I had it done?
Will I be able to have other children?
What will I feel like afterwards?
When I have children, will I remember?
How will I get time off work?
How will I pay for it?
What will my body be like afterwards?
Will I need a check-up?

Box 3.2

UPAA Statistics: Some Comments

In 1985 1,087 women from Northern Ireland went to Britain for abortions after having consulted with the UPAA. In 1986 the figure was 1,190, an increase of 93. Women aged 20 to 24 constitute the largest single group of those women. In 1985 they made up 34% and in 1986 38%. The most common referral source is the GP; in 1985 36% of women attending were referred by their GP, and in 1986 41%. Since 1980 referrals from GPs have increased from 29.8% to 41%.

In 1985 women under 17 constituted 5% of those coming to the UPAA, and in 1986 4%.

67% of the women attending in 1985 said they had used no contraceptive on the particular occasion they thought they had conceived. In 1986 this had risen to 70%. During January to December 1986 we asked all women coming to us if they had ever used contraception. 312 women said they had never done so, which is 26% of the total number of women having abortions through the UPAA.

Open Line Counselling

In addition to Northern Ireland referral agencies' evidence to the Tribunal, evidence was also presented by Open Line Counselling on the particular problems faced by women from the South in obtaining an abortion in England.

Open Line Counselling was established in July 1983 in response to the proven demand for a comprehensive, non-directive pregnancy counselling service. Its aims were:

to provide a supportive counselling and comprehensive referral service principally for pregnant women,
to provide information on women's health and sexuality, including pregnancy testing,
and to establish and maintain a network of contacts with workers in related medical, social and legal fields with training programmes for workers in the field.

Since July 1983, 2,000 women have been counselled, most of them Irish citizens, on unwanted pregnancies. The majority of these women (60%) were in the 20-29 age group, 79% were unmarried and 62% gave addresses outside of Dublin as their place of origin. Occupations included clerical and service workers (40%), professional workers, mainly nurses and teachers (12%), unemployed (7%) and full-time homemakers (15%). Of the women who chose to terminate their pregnancies, 64% did so before 12 weeks and a further 22% before 16 weeks. 39% of women had had at least one previous pregnancy, 11% had previously had an abortion and 6% had given a child for adoption. The pill and the condom remained the preferred method of contraception, with 36% of women reporting never having used any method of contraception.

The majority of women (61%) told their partners about their pregnancy and some women were accompanied by their partners when they attended counselling. Partners were described as boyfriend (68%), casual acquaintance (13%), husband (11%). By contrast the majority of women (63%) did not tell either family or friends. Friends were more likely to be told and to be supportive than family.

On the question of reasons for considering terminations, Open Line reported that

35

'a negative response to the pregnancy was common. Many younger women feel unprepared for a child, particularly where family and social support is unlikely or insufficient. Many women are also anxious to avoid causing hurt to their parents, especially where a parent has health problems. Older women are worried about the effects of another pregnancy on a grown family, and also about the possibility of a sub-normal child. Instability in the relationship with the putative father, whether casual, ex-boyfriend or where a marriage is under stress, is another common factor. Separated women with an extra-marital pregnancy are concerned about the irregular status of their relationship with the putative father and also about the threat to pregnancy. Professional women are increasingly concerned about their future training and employment prospects, particularly in nursing and teaching. Most women decide to seek termination because of a multiplicity of these pressures.'

Union of Students in Ireland

Where Open Line Counselling, from their position of dealing daily with women seeking abortions, was strong on statistical information, the evidence presented by the Union of Students in Ireland provided a sense of the personal experience of travelling to Britain for an abortion.

They stressed that for most women from the South of Ireland, and in particular for those with limited financial resources, the journey is done by boat and train, a long over-night experience. But, harrowing as this experience can be, it may even be tame compared with the situation to be found on the other side.

'Arrival is at London's Euston station at 6.15 a.m. After travelling all night and probably half the day previous without food, little money and fear of the unknown, she faces a gruelling day. The clinics do not open until 9.30 a.m. She has three and a half hours to wait in London. She cannot have breakfast. There is nowhere to sleep, nobody to go to. Chances are she will never have been in London before.

Arrival at the clinic—two large waiting rooms full of women, all with the same difficulty as her. Yes, there are Irish women too; one woman we helped met a woman from home! Both women experienced instantaneous horror; they both came from a small town in the west of Ireland. The shock, the dread— all for a second; two people, victims of a repressed state.

The counsellors with their awfully nice British accents, their apparent lack of understanding of the Irish mentality, mentality under seige. Sadly nowadays, the first time a woman will get advice on the options open to her will be an hour away from the operation in London.

Another wait, on to a bus with ten or fifteen others, to a nursing home where the operation will be performed. The traffic jams, the misted-up windows. On arrival at the home, a nurse checks the women in. There is another wait, more counselling, and then the anaesthetic.

8 p.m. that evening. The woman is awakened by the sounds of three or four other Irish women hazily wakening up to a feeling of disbelief. The nurse comes in with milky tea and digestives. Facing two or three other women in the ward; they are from Ireland too. They are sometimes young, sometimes in their thirties and forties, married and cannot cope with another child. There is a TV, sometimes a radio. The staff are friendly and visitors are allowed, not that anybody wants to talk. Sleep comes again.

At 8 a.m. the woman is discharged. Morning in London. The woman feels weak and drained. The Holyhead train leaves Euston at 10 p.m. that night—fourteen hours in London, nowhere to go, no money, and all she wants to do is sleep. The long train journey through the night, arriving in Holyhead at 2 a.m., cold, damp and tired, with the thoughts of the boat journey through the night. 6.30 a.m.—Dun Laoghaire. Back in Ireland.'

The British Pregnancy Advisory Service

In England, the majority of women from Northern Ireland will have their abortions in clinics which are non-profit making charities. One of these organisations, the British Pregnancy Advisory Service (BPAS), gave evidence to the Tribunal.

Two non-profit making charities were founded in 1968, one in Birmingham and the other in London, to advise women inquiring about termination of pregnancy under the new Abortion Act. Today, the London organisation continues to operate only in the Metropolitan area, but the Birmingham organisation, now named the British Pregnancy Advisory Service, has become a widespread service operating in England, Scotland and Wales.

The organisation has developed a range of professional services providing information, advice, counselling and treatment for any problem connected with pregnancy, contraception, male and female sterilisation and sub-fertility. It works through a network of local branches or counselling centres and five nursing homes registered under the terms of the Registered Homes Act 1984 and regulated under the terms of the Abortion Act 1967.

Counselling for unwanted pregnancy and abortion is still its main work, and each year BPAS provides: pregnancy testing for about 43,000 clients, counselling about pregnancy for about 25,000 clients, and abortion for about 24,000 patients.

BPAS services are necessarily part of the mixed economy of medical care but are not seen as a normal part of the private medical market or as a preferable alternative to care provided through the NHS for those who are prepared to pay. The NHS, however, meets less than half of the legally sanctioned demand for abortion from residents of England and Wales. In consequence, a majority of patients are coerced into paying for the service privately and are exposed to commercial exploitation of their distress. As long as NHS deficiencies prevail in the treatment of abortion, BPAS believes that it is in the public interest that the alternative private services that are needed should be in the hands of socially responsible organisations rather than in those of commercially motivated suppliers of facilities.

BPAS is inspired by the belief that all citizens should be enabled effectively to exercise their basic human right to control their own fertility by any of the means permitted by law, whether by avoiding unwanted pregnancy by contraception or sterilisation or by terminating an unwanted pregnancy. To this effect, BPAS, whilst only operating in Britain, sees women from Northern Ireland and has an interest in their welfare and treatment.

In Northern Ireland, the law, in the shape of the Abortion Act 1967, does not apply. Furthermore, in Britain where the Act is in force, the regulations deriving from the Act inhibit BPAS from responding more fully to the needs of Irish women. BPAS operates under Clause 1(3) of the Abortion Act 1967 which gives unlimited powers to Ministers to control advisory bureaux and nursing homes in the non-NHS sector wishing to be 'approved' for the termination of pregnancies, but has no relevance within the NHS. This control is exercised by the granting or withholding of a license to practice; there is no right of appeal and, inevitably, there has been a tendency to be more restrictive in the private sector. In certain ways, this had led to an improvement in standards of clinical practice, evidenced by authoritative publications from the Royal College of Obstreticians and Gynaecologists and the Royal College of General Practitioners. The regulations on the conduct of advisory bureaux and nursing homes prove very limiting to the dissemination of information and the accessibility of services for women in Northern Ireland.

Each BPAS centre is required to assure the Secretary of State that the following specific requirements will be complied with:

> 'There should be no advertising abroad either directly or indirectly and no association with any person or agency which advertises abroad;
> the nursing home must take proper and adequate precautions to avoid accepting any abortion patients as a result of advertising abroad even though the persons or agencies by whom the patients are referred may not have been directly involved in such practices; a nursing home must not admit abortion patients introduced or referred by or through persons or agencies abroad.'

The Secretary of State, for these purposes, has always regarded Northern Ireland as being 'abroad' and has not been prepared to differentiate in any way between Northern Ireland, Southern Ireland, Spain or any other country.

As stated, the regulations do not permit the distribution of any form of advertising material. This would include advice or information leaflets, for example, which carry the name and address of a BPAS or other nursing home. The regulations also frown on the known associations of BPAS with the Ulster Pregnancy Advisory Association and the Northern Ireland Family Planning Association.

However, advertising material such as notices in the Yellow Page Directories is now becoming common in Northern Ireland, stimulated by the more commercially motivated providers of services in England. The Secretary of State has not rescinded the regulations prohibiting this practice and it must be assumed that either he has given tacit approval by default, or he does not know!

BPAS has always fulfilled the regulations honestly in relation to advertising and information material. We have also, to a degree, duplicated in England the counselling and advisory services often provided by the Irish organisations. This has proved unwieldy, costly and more intrusive to the women involved in obtaining an abortion than should be necessary and we welcome this opportunity to expose the inadequacy of the present situation.

BPAS believes the Tribunal may wish to determine whether the slow erosion of regulation in this area by custom and practice is sufficient or whether a more radical approach should be recommended to the Secretary of State.

In addition to the costs associated with travel from Ireland and accommodation in England, the costs of counselling, assessment and the abortion operation create great difficulties for many women from Northern Ireland. BPAS maintains costs at the lowest level possible consistent with good quality of care and, being a charity with a positive policy to those women in genuine financial difficulties, we are probably more keenly aware of these problems than most.

There is no evidence from our data that Irish women with financial difficulties are a higher proportion of the total, but we can extend this finding in two ways. Firstly, where there is a financial problem, it is likely to be more profound. Secondly, communication difficulties tend to exacerbate the anxiety and problems the women have with their financial arrangements.

It is clear that, unlike Britain where BPAS can respond more easily to assist women where cost may be a factor in their decision concerning abortion, women arriving in England from Ireland for abortion have often had to reach their decision unsupported. It can only be speculation how many women have been forced into continuing with an unwanted pregnancy where cost has been a factor.

The majority of Northern Ireland women treated by BPAS are seen in Liverpool, and the degree to which clients in Liverpool are helped can be illustrated using 1986 data. 279 patients received treatment free or on a reduced fee basis, resulting in an investment by BPAS of £29,009 in non-applied charges. Some of this will have been subsequently repaid but from these audited accounts the situation is quite clearly demonstrated.

The BPAS concluded its evidence to the Tribunal by firmly supporting

'the extension of the Abortion Act 1967 to Northern Ireland. The relaxing of these regulations enacted in England and Wales that impact on the provision of services to women from Northern Ireland would be a valuable first step and we encourage the International Tribunal to make these recommendations.'

Box 3.3

BPAS and Office of Population Censuses and Surveys Statistics

Data from the Office of Population Censuses and Surveys indicates that approximately 1500 Northern Ireland women a year obtain an abortion in England and Wales. BPAS treats up to a third of all these women in Liverpool, the Midlands or Brighton.

Using BPAS records and the few official statistics that are available, a profile can be built up for 1985/86.

Age

The age distribution of residents of Northern Ireland correlates quite closely with residents of England and Wales being treated for abortion, with the exception of a slight bulge in the 20-24 age band. BPAS data on Northern Ireland women show a tendency for treatment to be provided to younger women as a proportion of the total.

Table 3.1: *Percentage distribution by age groups of women having abortions in Britain.*

	under 16	16 to 19	20 to 24	25 to 34	35 and over
Residents of England & Wales	2.8	24.2	29.8	30.6	12.6
Residents of NI	1.9	23.2	35.9	28.4	10.6
BPAS patients from NI	3.7	27.5	30.0	28.8	10.0

Gestation

Official statistics are not available routinely showing gestation of women from Northern Ireland, but OPCS figures illustrating non-residents of England and Wales as a total can be used for this purpose. Using this as a guide to the problems faced by women obtaining a more 'distant' service, there is a significantly higher proportion of women having late abortions.

BPAS data show a different pattern, where 86% of their abortions to Northern Ireland women are conducted in the first 12 weeks of pregnancy. This points more to the speed of response within BPAS rather than contradicting the more general findings, which is reinforced further when considered alongside the all-BPAS data where Northern Ireland women fare badly in the very early stages.

Table 3.2: *Gestation length (weeks) at time of abortion in Britain (percentages).*

	under 9	9 to 12	13 to 19	20 and over
Residents of England & Wales	34.1	52.6	11.8	1.5
Non-Residents of England & Wales	27.0	39.9	25.6	7.5
BPAS patients from NI	25.0	61.3	11.3	2.4

Liverpool Abortion Support Services

The Liverpool Abortion Support Services (LASS) gave evidence to the Tribunal on its care of women travelling from Ireland to Liverpool for abortions. The organisation was established when it became evident that numbers of Irish women were arriving in Liverpool for abortions and that

> 'it was apparent that for many women this was a traumatic experience made in financial hardship and in secret. Some women were found to be sleeping rough and many had no money to buy food for their journey home.'

41

In order to offer both practical and personal help, LASS set up a support scheme which offered accommodation and emotional support during the women's stay in Liverpool. They considered that the fact that LASS felt so strongly that there was such a need and the fact that this need has not abated in six years was surely evidence in itself for the extension of the 1967 Abortion Act to Northern Ireland.

Originally, because LASS was only a small group, they used the criterion of financial hardship for women being offered support. It was evident, however, that such hardship was true for the majority and the need for the scheme has continued to be such that this criterion is no longer stipulated. They would hope that any woman coming over would feel able to contact them.

LASS pointed to several worries gained through their first hand experience working with women in this situation.

1. Lack of medical care on the boat for women returning.
2. Lack of medical care available to many once home.
3. The emotional isolation for many coming in secret.
4. Being unable to discuss what should be a basic right for every woman and share feelings about this.
5. The financial strain this puts most women under. We have met women who have had to sell their belongings and others who have got into deep debt in order to come.
6. The fact of having no choice.

They concluded their evidence by reiterating that

'women do not undertake this decision lightly. They have made their decision for strong personal reasons and we respect every individual woman's choice. We are very concerned about what happens to women once they return home, but we cannot keep in touch because of the great need for confidentiality. We welcome the time when there will be no longer any need for groups such as LASS to exist. We support the sentiments of NIALRA and hope that the Tribunal can bring pressure to bear to have the same services available for women as there are in the rest of the UK.'

The Irish Women's Abortion Support Group

Another support group which gave evidence to the Tribunal was the Irish Women's Abortion Support Group, a voluntary group made up of Irish women and second generation Irish women. Officially since 1981, and informally before that, it has existed to give Irish women practical and emotional help when they arrive in England for an abortion. First contact is by telephone (031-251 6332/3 or 031-490 0042, between 6 p.m. and 9 p.m. on Tuesdays). The Group pointed out that

'many women ring us from public call boxes, and, as the line is constantly busy, they often have to wait hours before getting through. Women have often travelled miles to the next town in order to avoid detection—and that after having made numerous calls throughout Ireland before finally getting our number. They are frequently in tears on the phone, some talking for the first time about their unwanted pregnancy, crying because they want to have an abortion and they cannot openly talk about it in the present social climate. For these women it is tremendously important that we are Irish women who support them in their decision and help them to come to terms with it.'

They told the Tribunal of the case of one woman, Eilis, who was

'at the end of her tether. She was 26 years old and still living at home. She had a part-time job as a cleaner. She had been raped by her brother-in-law while babysitting. She was told by her GP that she was 18 weeks pregnant at the time of her phone call, although she knew the date of the rape to have been earlier. She had been trying to save up for the abortion and had been putting it off until she thought she had enough money. Although she didn't have enough money saved, we told her that it was best if she came as soon as possible and that we would act as guarantor if she would pay back the outstanding cost after her abortion.

She told her mother that she was going to Tralee for the weekend and that she would stay with a friend. She had to be back on Monday so that she could look after her mentally handicapped sister while her mother attended a funeral. When she arrived off the plane, one of us went to meet her and brought her to the clinic. During the consultation, it was discovered that she was in fact 22 weeks pregnant, which meant that she would have to be booked into another clinic. Luckily for Eilis another clinic could take her; however, her abortion would cost a hundred pounds more and she would have to stay an extra day. Not only had she the worry of the abortion itself, but also the extra cost and more particularly the repercussions she would face when she got home.'

The number of women contacting the group has grown rapidly since the Hamilton ruling led to the closing of the referral agencies in Dublin.

'The majority of women who contact us are unemployed or in receipt of other social welfare allowances. If they're lucky, they have a part-time job, but whatever the circumstances, the cost of travel and the abortion is a great burden.'

Worst off of all are the women who

'come over on spec, hoping that once they reach London they would find out where to go. In these instances they have been vulnerable to rip-offs by taxi drivers and clinics.'

The Irish Women's Abortion Support Group ended their evidence by repeating the importance of Irish women being able to contact other Irish women who were supportive. This helps them to realise that they are not as isolated as they feel. But the cost of such support, not least in financial terms, is a severe drain on the Group.

4.

Women's Groups

Introduction

In preparation for the International Tribunal the organisers wrote to women's groups throughout Northern Ireland requesting them to present evidence. In particular they were asked to assess whether or not the women they were dealing with on a daily basis experienced a need for abortion facilities in Northern Ireland and how they were affected by the lack of such facilities. In the event six groups responded to the call for evidence, namely:

the Well Woman Centre,
the Northern Ireland Women's Rights Movement,
the Falls Women's Centre,
Rape and Incest Line,
the Rape Crisis Centre, and
Lesbian Line.

It should be pointed out that, although these groups are all based in Belfast, they do in fact serve the needs of women all over Northern Ireland and offer their services province-wide. They can therefore legitimately claim to reflect the views of large numbers of women throughout Northern Ireland and not those of Belfast alone.

Five of these groups submitted evidence to the Tribunal; one did not, and sent an apology. The five which did submit all supported unreservedly the call for the provision of legal abortion facilities locally in Northern Ireland. They based this squarely on actual experience of the problem in the lives of the women encountered in the day-to-day work of their centres.

It is this latter aspect which makes the submissions from the women's groups important and in a sense unique; it is the human face of the statistics.

Each group reported experiences of the problem of women seeking termination of unwanted pregnancies.

The Well Woman Centre

The Well Woman Centre stated that

> 'while we do not exist, in any sense, specifically as an abortion referral service, our experience is that inquiries concerning

abortion are one of the most constant—and increasing—areas of women's needs with which we have to deal.'

Consequently, they reported an increasing rate of women contacting the Centre for information regarding termination of pregnancy, going on a rising scale from six in the first month in which the Centre was open to three or four a week in the last weeks of the year July 1986-July 1987. The Well Woman Centre's representative said:

'We do not know the results of all these calls and it is difficult to maintain contact because of the social pressures which enforce an unnatural silence and need of confidentiality upon the women. But we know that at least 40% proceeded with a termination, in each case having to find the money and "accountable" time to travel to England and back.'

She felt very strongly that as

'the overall well-being of women is the *raison d'etre* of a Well Woman Centre, we cannot but protest at any situation, legal or otherwise, which is the cause of such exacerbation of distress as this.'

The Northern Ireland Women's Rights Movement

The Northern Ireland Women's Rights Movement stated that

'most of the inquiries which we have handled have involved women in their teens or early twenties who are single and do not have the adequate financial means to travel to England to get an abortion. However, women have also come to us who have different domestic situations and of varying age groups.'

They also felt that, given that 'traditional negative attitudes to illegitimacy still prevail here', and other 'social factors such as the lack of sex education in schools and the general lack of information on contraception', there will undoubtedly be an even greater rise in the number of Irish women seeking abortions in England. They concluded:

'It stands as an indictment of the society in which we live that there is a flat refusal to extend the 67 Act to Northern Ireland.'

Rape and Incest Line

Rape and Incest Line, a group dealing with sexual violence, spoke of the women who find themselves pregnant as a result of sexual violation. They felt that it is crucially important in their work to try to give women some sense of control over their own lives, and this is not helped when the woman decides on an abortion only to find that she is denied this.

'No woman decides to have an abortion lightly; it is a long and agonising decision. However, once that decision has been made, why make it so difficult that often arranging the abortion itself can be another nightmare?'

They conclude:

> 'Surely, instead of continually hammering the victim, we should be thinking of changing a system to encourage more open discussion about sexuality, together with a structured and efficient and caring sexual education programme. We should be offering support and understanding to those women who feel that for them there is no alternative to abortion, instead of brutalising them still further.'

The Rape Crisis Centre

The Rape Crisis Centre began by attacking the myth that women do not become pregnant as a result of rape. But the bulk of their testimony was in relation to the 1987 Criminal Injuries (Northern Ireland) Order, which contains the following clause:

> 'If the victim sustains an injury directly attributable to rape and has given birth to a child conceived as a result of the rape and the victim intends to keep the child, an additional £5,000 will be payable.'

However, a further clause makes that payment dependent on the moral judgments of the awarding body:

> 'In assessing compensation, the character and way of life of the victim or applicant will be taken into account.'

The Rape Crisis Centre representative concluded that

> 'the fact that in Northern Ireland the state does not give women the choice of free, safe, legal abortion yet offers the paltry sum of £5,000 (with the aforementioned conditions) toward the upkeep of a child the woman did not choose to have is a gross insult to all women.'

Finally, she noted the important links between the Rape Crisis Centre and the Family Planning Association and the Ulster Pregnancy Advisory Association, but said that

> 'the absence of the 1967 Abortion Act allows individual health workers to include their own moral attitude with—and thus effectively censor—any advice they give women regarding the "morning after pill", the coil, or reliable abortion information.'

Lesbian Line

Lesbian Line

> 'has received calls from women who have had an unwanted pregnancy ... Some women have known that they wanted an abortion. Others have just wanted to have information on how to get an abortion, so that they can feel more empowered to make the right decision for themselves. Yet others have not considered

abortion as an option for them at all. Only when all options, including the option of abortion, are freely available, can a woman make a decision based on her own situation. No one can know the situation better than the woman herself, and whatever decision she makes deserves our full support.'

The spokeswoman for Lesbian Line also emphasised that the present financial cost often ensures that abortion is not available as a realistic option for many women.

Conclusion

A number of constant factors were clearly recurrent in the evidence of each group, yet each had independently isolated those factors from their own separate experiences of working with women. These factors were perhaps best exemplified in a series of points set out by the Well Woman Centre as evidence of the need to extend the 1967 Act to Northern Ireland.

1. The dangers to women of lack of proper medical care, *etc* before and after the operation. Women returning to Northern Ireland frequently have no chance of genuine medical care, certainly not care given in a non-judgmental atmosphere. What woman wants to willingly submit herself to what could become yet another ordeal?

2. The incurring of debts through being unable to afford travel and accommodation costs on top of clinic fees, and the loss of earnings through being off work, as well as the stress consequent on this. Here we have the class discrimination imposed by money, which should be totally unacceptable if the principle is equal health care for all.

3. The dangers of opting through despair for illegal operations in trying to avoid all the hassles involved in travel, costs and time, plus loss of earnings.

4. The psychological and emotional stress of having to travel alone and to cope with everything alone, because the whole situation so often has to be hidden, thus causing the deprivation of support and the human need to share a problem. Returning to a situation where the experience cannot be coped with through discussion and the articulation of feelings, the 'externalisation' of the trauma which is necessary for recovery. Instead, these feelings are repressed and will fester or find outlet in other, negative ways.

5. The anxiety and personal sense of affront in having been involved in something seen as 'illegal'—the law enshrining a moralistic and corporate judgment in what is, and ought to be, a personal and individual assessment, thus creating a ready-made atmosphere of apportioning 'blame', where understanding is what is required. A law which 'forbids' abortion is setting the tone for this sense of social wrong-doing with which the woman must contend repeatedly as though she were a criminal, sustaining devastating

emotional and psychological damage in consequence.

Above all, the evidence of the women's groups made clear that there was a stark gap between the typical stereotype so frequently portrayed of the woman seeking a pregnancy termination—the 'promiscuous' teenager, who is easily put forward as ready for censure and regarded as disgusting, deservedly reaping due rewards for her 'bad' conduct, *etc*— *and* the reality of the woman seeking termination, as experienced by women's groups who actually meet women in this situation—a woman who is married, has three or four children already, whose husband has left her and does not support them regularly. He comes back unexpectely, there is a brief reunion, the unresolved problems which parted them in the first place flare up again and he leaves, again. Six weeks later the woman finds she is pregnant; she tries to contact the man; he does not want to know and refuses to accept responsibility. The woman has, and desperately needs, the part-time job with which she can barely manage to support them all now; this will also go if she continues with the pregnancy. All the women's groups will know which of these is the realistic scenario and the one where the maximum problems and despair will ensue. As the spokeswoman for the Well Woman Centre put it:

> 'We who work with "ordinary" women every day of the week would protest vigourously against the sordid depiction of women who seek abortion; the woman considering abortion is not a dirty, shameless hussy or a bad woman or a stupid fool or a slag or a murderess. She is just a woman who finds herself pregnant at the wrong time and in the wrong circumstances to allow her to be what any woman would want to be at such a time—a good and loving mother.'

5.

Women Speaking

Introduction

The panel members received evidence from women from Northern Ireland who had had abortions, all but one of them outside Northern Ireland. That evidence was in two forms. Firstly, in an 'evidence pack' which all panel members received were the transcripts of interviews with a number of women. Secondly, during the two days of the International Tribunal the panel members heard the verbal evidence of a number of women; some of these women had already been interviewed and their transcripts submitted, while others were providing evidence for the first time. In the case of both the oral testimony and the transcripts, the evidence was not made public at the Tribunal, but was available to the panel members only.

In compiling this report, it was felt necessary to include the thoughts of at least some of the people about whom the whole International Tribunal was in fact about, the women from Northern Ireland who have had abortions. Consequently, with the permission of the women concerned, this chapter contains excerpts from the transcripts of the interviews with five women.

Their stories tell of confusion and yet relief, of loneliness and yet support. Above all, they confirm the points made by the women's groups and the referral and support agencies—the extra trauma of not being able to have access to legal, safe and supportive abortion services here in Northern Ireland, and the hypocrisy of a society which exports its abortion problem while demanding complete silence about the issue.

Witness A

In early April 1985 I suspected I was pregnant as my period was long overdue. I decided to have a test done.

At the time I was working in a Belfast city centre shop. As I had a short lunch break, the only place I could get to go for a test was the Life counselling office in Bryson House. Under the pretence of being married, I got the test done. It was positive. I went home and broke all the news to my boyfriend, whom I have been together with for nine years. He was really supportive and never interfered with my decision making. We considered all possibilities, but as both our families are deeply religious, the idea of a pregnancy would have caused huge

49

The difficult part for me was trying to get to London and trying to arrange travel without anybody knowing. It was totally secretive. I told nobody except the people I directly had to implicate to help me by looking after my children. So I had to leave my children. I had to find the money to pay for the termination and get the money for the fare. And the man I was involved with shared the cost with me, and it was all very distressing because he didn't want me to go.

I went on my own and you were allowed into the clinic early in the evening. They allowed women who were coming from Ireland to stay overnight and a lot of people had to get bed and breakfast, so I was saved that. I stayed that night and then the next morning I was up very early and sat around for a bit and then went to the clinic. And they were very kind. All that side of it went very humanely; I was treated very kindly and when I woke up, I was in a ward with about six or eight other women and the staff were very supportive and nice. And I just remember feeling this incredible sense of relief! Total and complete relief! I can't remember how long I stayed there. All I can remember is this really clear image of going out of that place and walking down the street and feeling such a burden lifted off me. It was great, I really felt so relieved.

So then I came back and it was peculiar. I couldn't say to anyone where I'd been. And I found it quite difficult emotionally during the next months, having had children. I think the worst thing is knowing other people's attitudes to it and realising that, if your family knew, you'd be disowned completely. Also, I was in a group of women who were talking about it. Somebody came into the group and read a poem which they said their daughter had brought home from school and a friend of hers had written. But I don't think it was. I think it was planted by Life, because it was a poem from the point of view of a foetus about six weeks old which was about to be aborted, and it was horrendous. And people said, 'Oh, that's terribly sad', and I was just devestated by it. You know, just the sense that all the people in that room, had they known, would have considered me a murderer. And I couldn't say. So what I said was, 'How do you think it would feel for a woman that had been to England and had had an abortion and was sitting in this room, faced with your reaction?' And they just said, 'Well, I suppose she would feel very guilty.' And I said, 'Yeah, she would feel very guilty and very isolated and unhappy.' And we had a discussion about it and by the end of the discussion people were saying, 'Well, I don't agree with abortion, but I believe it should be a woman's right to choose.' And it was peculiar because I was arguing, as it were, from a statistical point of view and yet I was arguing for myself. It struck me that maybe there is more support if you talk on a one-to-one or in a small group rather than confronting women with the ideological arguments.

The other thing that did have an effect on me is that I did go for a check-up to the family planning clinic six weeks afterwards because I was very concerned that I shouldn't get an infection. And I felt a strong sense that I was disapproved of. I don't know whether it was my own

50

problems and certain isolation from both families, and neither or us wanted to have a forced marriage. I had no hope of continuing my job, and finally, I was not ready to make the commitment of starting a family.

Next problem was arranging time off work. Special reasons had to be given for requesting Saturdays off work. As I was travelling by ferry, I needed the Friday off also. The story was 'a wedding of a friend in London'.

The next four weeks were agonizing ones. My conscious moments were filled with thoughts of, 'Should I or shouldn't I?', knowing all the time I really didn't want to go through with the pregnancy.

By the time I set off with my friend on Thursday night to Liverpool I was sure I was doing the right thing. First port of call was the clinic for a counselling session to ascertain if I was sure. Were they kidding? I was positively positive! Then visits to various nurses and doctors for tests and form filling.

Next problem was to find accommodation for the night. Whilst in the clinic I discovered I wasn't the only one from the North or even from County Down. A twenty year old girl was there with her *granny*. So we suggested sharing the cost of a taxi and looked for rooms together. We got fixed up in a nearby hotel which did cheaper rates for those attending the clinic.

Once settled in the ward on Saturday, I found three other women in the ward were from the South of Ireland, and the fourth from Liverpool. The Irish girls like myself had travelled under secrecy and had spent huge amounts of money to get to Liverpool. We all discussed our 'case histories' and were great support to each other. We had some good laughs too. The operations were all done on Saturday afternoon. By the time Sunday morning arrived and bags were packed, I felt a great sense of relief and was looking forward to carrying on as normal when I got home.

I was back at work Monday morning, but rested up as much as possible in the days that followed. As time passed I thought of the whole experience less and less. However, when abortion has since been mentioned, I would love to have said, 'Oh, I had one done'. But the consequences I felt that would follow have always kept me quiet.

Witness B

It was at Christmas four years ago, when I was 34, that I became pregnant by accident. I came back home and was talking to the man whom I was involved with, the potential father. It was very difficult because he desperately wanted me to have his child. But I knew that I just couldn't cope with it at all; everything in me rejected the idea of having a child. I just knew that as a single parent and working that I just could not go through with it. Which was a surprise because my previous pregnancies had been really positive and healthy and I really loved being pregnant. So I found that very difficult to cope with.

imagination; it wasn't expressed as disapproval, it was expressed as extreme discomfort. It just didn't seem as if they could handle it in the family planning clinic.

It cost an awful lot of money. I was fortunate. I was very fortunate that I was working at that time. If I hadn't been working, I would have had to borrow the money and maybe that would have involved implicating myself in either telling more people or borrowing money from the bank, and it would have been much harder. So, anybody who doesn't have money would find it almost impossible. Then there's the strain of travelling to a strange place without friends to comfort and support you. And in my case, the anxiety of leaving my children. It was a very painful decision, and one that I hope never to have to make again.

Witness C

I was 22 at the time, had graduated and had started working full-time. I had had a couple of long-term relationships before I was 21, one of which was when I had made the commitment to start using the pill, and, when that relationship ended, I decided that for me, at that stage in my life, to stay on the pill wasn't the right thing. What happened thereafter was that I met a man that I knew and who I had been very friendly with and I ended up having sexual intercourse. Out of that I conceived, though I was never able to approach him, in that it was a casual relationship and I was still friends with him, but didn't want it to go any further.

So then I decided that I had to do something. I couldn't at that stage have coped with having a child and went about organising it for myself. There were two people whom I confided in, both of whom were men, one of whom was actually very supportive to me, although he was very curious to know who the person was who would have been the father of the child if I had been full term, but I refused. On that I held my privacy and confidence.

So, one afternoon in work I got the phone number for the Liverpool Clinic and phoned them up and booked myself in and booked the boat. The story at home, because at that stage I was living at home with my parents, was I was going over to visit my sister in Manchester, because that was where she was working. My story to my sister in Manchester was that I was going to stay with her for two nights, but I was going to this conference in Liverpool, so that I would not have to stay with her for one night. So there was that cloak of secrecy around it all and I didn't feel I could, nor did I want to, confide in my family.

I had to make a day trip to Liverpool to go through the pre-op preliminaries and I am a great one for hiding behind things and for being active, and I remember my knitting went with me and I was doing the most complicated thing I have ever knit in my whole life and that was my company, for when I got to the reception, I found that everyone had someone with them and I had my knitting. I was giving the impression that I was independent; all you people stay off, because I can cope. There was a big counselling session with one of the workers. The counsellor was great. I didn't have to be coping on my own, I didn't have to be 100% okay, it was all right to feel anxious and nervous about it.

So then I went back down to Manchester and stayed that night with my sister and had to come up the next day. I haven't any great memories of the next day except not having to eat and all that. One thing I do remember was that prior to when the general anaesthetic happened, the nurse had her mask on and she had her eyes made up fantastically; they were gorgeous. That is the last memory I had. I just found that so comforting, which is surprising for someone who never wears make-up, these gorgeously made-up eyes and her stroking my hand. It was a really nice way to go off into this anaesthetic. The waking up was just awful, not in terms of guilt, but just the surroundings were awful. Everybody else was just so relieved to have it over and I remember thinking 'what the hell am I doing lying here? This is just horrible; it's just so uncomfortable. I don't like this place.' And the attitude of the staff was not great, and I wanted to be away.

Then they brought us round the tea and toast and when they allowed me to get up, I went and phoned the other male friend in Belfast, talked to him, because I really needed that link and that support, because everyone else seemed to have someone and I was feeling very isolated. I found this bit really unsettling and then I got talking to a number of the women there at the clinic who were from Northern Ireland and then ended up travelling back with a girl who was from County Down and remember her being so relieved. And her boyfriend had come and met her, so there was actually the three of us who went back together. I was met off the boat and brought back up to my mother's and had to do the 'it was really nice being in Manchester' routine.

It was going for the six weeks' check-up ... hating that ... just hating that. The attitude of the people was really very schoolmarmish and very judgmental towards me. No attempt to try and understand what I had been through, why I had been through it, what had got me to that stage, just incredibly judgmental and clinical and 'let's get the job done', that made me even more draw into myself rather than come out. I went to the Family Planning Clinic for it. I could have gone to my own GP but didn't. I know the abortion is on my record and that every time I go along to the clinic that it's there and that it's seen and I feel uncomfortable with that.

Witness D

I was 18. It was my last year in the Upper Sixth and I was just about to do my A-level exams. I had had two negative pregnancy tests which I paid for myself, but, even though I had been given these negative results, because I didn't have a period, I knew that I must be pregnant. Finally I went to my family doctor and had a test done there. I phoned up for the result on the day I was doing my Geography A-level exam. We didn't have a phone in the house, so I had to go to the local shop because the public phone box had been vandalised as usual. The only phone I could use was in the local butcher's, which was a strange place to have to go. I remember phoning and praying and hoping that I was going to get a negative result and that would be it, then being told it was positive over the phone and trying to get out of the shop and contain myself. This happened in the morning and I had to go to school that afternoon and sit down and start writing about stupid Geography questions, when all the time I kept thinking about what the hell I was going to do.

I was living with my mum. We had somebody staying with us at the time. She had come back from London and, because she had been out of Northern Ireland, her views were a bit more liberal. And I told her, and she told me to have hot baths, and she also told me that I could maybe do it myself with soap and told me to shave down my soap. And so I tried this and developed the shakes all over because the bath was so hot. I tried bouncing down stairs and all sorts of crazy things, but of course nothing happened. She told my mother even though I had told her not to, and my mum then was terribly upset.

My mum phoned a friend of the family. He had actually been our minister at some stage, though he was no longer our minister, and I went to see him. He arranged for me to see a doctor in the City Hospital and I again had a pregnancy test and again it was positive. And I received some counselling from a very young psychiatrist who explained to me that the only way I could receive an abortion in Northern Ireland under the present legislation was for me to appear to be totally devastated, in such a way that I was going to have a nervous breakdown if the pregnancy continued ,and went through questions that I would be asked by a gynaecologist and another psychiatrist. He told me there were certain answers that I shouldn't give for I would sound far too rational. He told me not to use arguments like 'I didn't plan to be pregnant, I don't want to have a baby', because that sounded too rational, and also not to express any doubt about what I was doing. It was very confusing and I felt very powerless, very frightened.

The next thing was to arrange that I saw a gynaecologist. I had to sit for hours, but I finally went in to see this gynaecologist who examined me and said that I was 14 weeks pregnant. This absolutely terrified me because anything I had read about abortions in England had suggested that after 12 weeks it wasn't really on. It was getting more dangerous. I suddenly felt that there was a conspiracy against me, that they were saying I was 14 weeks pregnant and it was so as they would now be able to give medical reasons why I couldn't have an abortion, and that I had been really tricked into this situation, that it was false security that I was going to be helped. I remember jumping down off the examining couch and saying that, if they weren't going to give me an abortion, I was going out to do it myself right now, and running out of this room, some nurse trying to restrain me, and somehow managing to throw people off and get out onto the Lisburn Road and walking from there home.

Then this friend of the family, the minister, came round again and asked me to go and see the doctor who had first seen me, and she talked to me again and she asked if I was absolutely sure, had I considered adoption, and really went over all the options. I was really absolutely terrified at the thought that I was going to have to have a baby and then have the baby adopted. I just could not imagine doing that. She said: 'We have arranged for you to go into hospital', so that was all right. I was to go and pack a case. I went to another hospital to a gynaecological ward and was, very, very luckily, actually placed in a side ward. It was very kind of them to arrange for me to be in a side ward, but you know what women's wards are like. You are not left on your own. So there were women who would come in and talk to me and I had to pretend that I had fibroids and that was what I was worried about, because I was doing a lot of crying. I had been through so many questioning sessions and I felt so guilty about wanting to have an abortion, yet I was absolutely terrified of the thought of having to have a baby when I didn't want to have a baby, and I spent a lot of time crying and really feeling terribly helpless, depending so much on the good will of these doctors and whether or not they would help me.

Then there was another gynaecological examination and this time it was a younger doctor. He examined me and he said that I was 17 weeks pregnant. Then the consultant who examined me and said I was 14 weeks pregnant came in and said, 'Well, you must be at least 14, possibly 17 weeks pregnant. You realise that this will mean we can't do an abortion by the vaginal method. We will have to do a hysterotomy.' He explained that this would entail having to cut through to the uterus and remove the foetus by that method. He also said that doing this would undoubtedly weaken the uterine wall and it could cause difficulty in my carrying a child to full term in later life and that there was a high risk that I might be very prone to miscarriage after this procedure had been carried out. He asked me if I was still determined to go ahead with the abortion and I said yes, I was. And as soon as he left, I just could not stop crying because I hadn't imagined not having children at some stage in my life, but I definitely didn't want to have a baby then. The thought of doing something to my body that would prevent me from ever having children was really terrible. Then a psychiatrist was brought in to see me and the psychiatrist put me through all these questions about how I felt and made some remark about me having a very feminine psychology and then went off and said I was not to worry, that everything would be all right.

I don't exactly know how they managed to make it okay that I had the abortion which I did have. I remember coming out of the anaesthetic and the first thing I did was ask had I an incision across my stomach and being told that I hadn't, that it had been all right, that it hadn't been necessary, and being so relieved, just being so totally relieved. I had to go back to the theatre again and have another D and C because I bled very heavily after the abortion and that was pretty awful—two general anaesthetics within a matter of days.

It was terrible the way it had to be so undercover. I know it had to be undercover because it's illegal in Northern Ireland to have an abortion. I know the doctors who helped me were taking a great risk and I don't know how in the end they justified it. They must have used psychiatric reasons, that I was really unstable. In talking to me they hadn't actually said what they were going to write down on the piece of paper, so I never knew. I don't know if it is on some record somewhere that I was about to self-destruct, that I would have committed suicide. Actually, the way I felt, I would have done something fairly desperate, but it was because of the situation I was in. I don't think I was being particularly irrational. I didn't want to have a baby. I hadn't planned to have a baby and I was asking for the right not to have to bring a child into the world that I didn't want.

Witness E

It was just before my 31st birthday that I found myself pregnant. My baby was only 10 months and I couldn't remember having had intercourse without protection. I was always very careful, given that I had faced an unwanted pregnancy before and I had had an abortion when I was still living abroad.

After delivery I had gone through a long period of 'baby blues'. I love my partner and our child, but being tied to the house is something I had never experienced before, and it took a long time of adjustment. However, the breastfeeding period was over, I was free to go but there was no job. I have a whole file full of applications from only 3 or 4 months of trying; it surely isn't easy here. But I didn't give up, I knew I'd find something. So I was just getting optimistic again, just getting out of those dull feelings of having nothing to show for a full day's work, having no social life, with all my friends working during the day, and not even having found a mother's and toddler's group that I felt at home with. So I was just about to get out of my depression when it happened.

It feels a long time ago now although it isn't all that long. I remember the nights of discussion, but it didn't take long to decide. I contacted the UPAA. I knew that abortion is illegal in Northern Ireland but I also knew that some are performed, and I just wanted to be among those some. All my inquiries gave the same answer: 'You have no chance'. I got annoyed and frustrated. I had had an abortion abroad which had been no problem, local anaesthetic and out I was two hours later, feeling fine and relieved. Why couldn't I have the same here? Why did I have to go to England? What threw me off completely was to learn that I wouldn't be allowed local anaesthetic when going to England. I would have to stay at least two overnights, the operation being done the day in between under full anaesthetic. I must say that I hate anaesthetics and I am frightened of a full one, so I ran up our phone bill phoning clinics in London, trying to find one that would take me in under local anaesthetic. No luck. I got more and more frustrated, didn't know where to go. I finally remembered I still had the name of the doctor who had performed my abortion before. He had been my ordinary 'Woman's GP', as they call it, a gynaecologist you register with for check-ups and smears, *etc*, just like you register with a GP. So I phoned him and asked could I not get an abortion on the international form, E111 or whatever you call it. He said he didn't think that was possible, but no matter what, I should come straight away.

I was seven weeks pregnant when I booked my flight and in the eighth week when the operation was done. So I had just about been early enough, because doctors are only allowed to perform an abortion in their surgeries up to and including 8 weeks duration. I got my local anaesthetic and walked out without problems; my 'old' doctor had been very sympathetic, he didn't charge me a penny. Going to the continent ended up half as expensive as it would have been for me to go to England because I did not have to pay for the operation or any accommodation. I am very grateful to the doctor, I wish there were more like him, understanding and acting accordingly.

There is one point I would like to make, which is that for me the first and the second abortion were a totally different experience. The first time I could share my situation, my feelings and fears with my friends, which I could not do this time round. I don't know if you can imagine what it is like having to hide before relatives and friends, having always to try to imagine their reactions first, without being able to just walk up and tell them. Nobody outside our relationship knew where I was and what I was doing. Of course it was a problem to hide my being away for a whole week. But the worst of all was the feeling that this created in me, the feeling of doing something wrong, illegal, criminal.

I am not from here and I have never thought that way about abortion. But the secrecy I felt I had to operate under automatically made me doubt and, realising that, I got very angry. My experience helped me understand how hard a burden it must be for any woman from here who has not been brought up in a more liberal attitude such as I was, to make up her mind and go through with it. How determined must they be!

Having gone through two experiences of an unwanted pregnancy in two different countries myself I am in the 'fortunate' situation to be able to compare. I prefer the more liberal attitude I found abroad and I am sure that extending the 67 Abortion Act to Northern Ireland will not only prevent unnecessary hardship and suffering (and expense!) but in the long run will also help to create a more liberal atmosphere: a society in which abortion is not a taboo, in which sexuality and contraception are more freely discussed and where then—through re-education and change of attitudes (for example towards contraception!)—hopefully there will be a lesser need for abortions.

6.

Legal Evidence

Madge Davison, Law Lecturer at Queen's University Belfast, outlined the legal situation regarding abortion in Northern Ireland. She began by stating that the law on abortion in Northern Ireland is very different from the rest of the United Kingdom and that it is much more restrictive. The law is criminal in nature and stems primarily from statute law and the common law.

The 1861 Offences Against the Person Act

As regards statute law, she first considered the 1861 Offences Against the Person Act and explained that, despite the 1967 Abortion Act in England, this piece of Victorian legislation remains operative, not only in Northern Ireland but in all parts of the UK. The 1967 Act did not repeal the 1861 Offences Against the Person Act; it merely stated those situations in which abortion would henceforth be legal (see Box 1).

Box 6.1

Excerpt from the 1967 Abortion Act

Sections 1.1 and 5.1 of the 1967 Abortion Act read as follows:

1.1 'Subject to the provisions of this section, a person shall not be guilty of an offence under the law relating to abortion when a pregnancy is terminated by a registered medical practitioner if two registered medical practitioners are of the opinion, formed in good faith,

(a) that the continuance of the pregnancy would involve risk to the life of the pregnant woman, or of injury to the physical or mental health of the pregnant woman or any existing children of her family, greater than if the pregnancy were terminated; or
(b) that there is a substantial risk that if the child were born it would suffer from such physical or mental abnormalities as to be seriously handicapped.

5.1 Nothing in this Act shall affect the provisions of the Infant Life (Preservation) Act 1929 (protecting the life of the viable foetus).

The Offences Against The Person Act (see Box 6.2) outlaws 'unlawful' abortions. Given that most Acts of Parliament, when passed, have definition sections to clarify what certain sections mean, Ms. Davison argued, it was most interesting that within the 1861 Act there is no such section. It talks about people 'unlawfully' procuring a miscarriage or 'unlawfully' administering poison, but there is no definition of the word 'unlawful'.

It must be assumed, she argued, that some abortions must have been perceived to have been lawful. She supported her argument by quoting the fact that quite a number of legal writers have subsequently stated that Parliament deliberately used the term 'unlawful'. Ms. Davison believes it has probably been established as a common law notion from time immemorial that abortions were possible in extreme emergencies to save the life of the woman. She therefore sees the 1861 Act, although it never explicitly stated this, to recognise cases where abortions would be lawful and that these would probably be cases of severe risk to the life of the mother.

Box 6.2

Excerpt from the 1861 Offences Against the Person Act

The Offences Against the Person Act became law on November 1, 1861. It contains 79 paragraphs and covers a wide range of possible offences, including:

administering poison,
destroying or damaging a building with gunpowder,
setting fire to or casting away a ship with intent to murder,
sending letters threatening to murder,
impeding a person endeavouring to save himself from shipwreck,
not providing apprentices and servants with food,
placing wood on a railway with intent to endanger passengers,
driving a carriage furiously,
obstructing a clergyman in the discharge of his duties,
assaulting a magistrate,
assault with intent to obstruct the sale of grain,
assaulting a seaman,
asssaulting females and boys under fourteen years old,
rape,
carnal knowledge of a girl under ten years of age,
abduction of a girl under age against her father's will,
forcible abduction of a woman with intent to marry her,
child stealing,
bigamy,
sodomy and bestiality,
concealing the birth of a child.

In the midst of this are two paragraphs on abortion. They read, in full, as follows:

> '58. Every Woman, being with Child, who, with Intent to procure her own Miscarriage, shall unlawfully administer to herself any Poison or other noxious Thing, or shall unlawfully use any Instrument or other Means whatsoever with the like Intent, and whosoever, with Intent to procure the Miscarriage of any Woman, whether she be or be not with Child, shall unlawfully administer to her or cause to be taken by her any Poison or other noxious Thing, or shall unlawfully use any Instrument or other Means whatsoever with the like Intent, shall be guilty of Felony, and being convicted thereof shall be liable, at the Discretion of the Court, to be kept in Penal Servitude for Life, or for any Term, not less than Three Years—or to be imprisoned for any Term not exceeding Two Years, with or without Hard Labour, and with or without Solitary Confinement.
>
> 59. Whosoever shall unlawfully supply or procure any Poison or other noxious Thing, or any instrument or Thing whatsoever, knowing that the same is intended to be unlawfully used or employed with Intent to procure the Miscarriage of any Woman, whether she be or be not with Child, shall be guilty of a Misdemeanour, and being convicted thereof shall be liable, at the Discretion of the Court, to be kept in Penal Servitude for the Term of Three Years, or to be imprisoned for any Term not exceeding Two Years, with or without Hard Labour.'

The Infant Life (Preservation) Act

This was the state of the law until 1929 in England, when the Infant Life (Preservation) Act was passed. Northern Ireland was excluded from the provisions of that Act until 1945 when it was subsequently enacted for Northern Ireland as the Criminal Justice (Northern Ireland) Act.

The contents of the 1929 Act (and subsequently the Criminal Justice Act of 1945), were briefly summarised by Ms. Davison. They state that any person who with intent destroys the life of a child capable of being born alive is guilty of a felony, that is, child destruction, the penalty for which is penal servitude for life.

Ms. Davison pointed out that an interesting proviso was added in this Act. It provided that no person be found guilty under the Act unless it was proved that the act which caused the death of the child was not done in good faith for the purpose only of preserving the life of the mother (see Box 6.3). It was very interesting that this was included, because the 1861 Act did not talk about acting to preserve the life of the mother. Only in common law could we presume that abortions could be performed in an emergency. This was the first time any condition or situational exceptance had been written into the statute books.

Box 6.3

Excerpts from the 1929 Infant Life (Preservation) Act

The 1929 Infant Life (Preservation) Act, article 1.1 states:

'Subject as hereinafter in this subsection provided, any person who, with intent to destroy the life of a child capable of being born alive, by any wilful act causes a child to die before it has an existence independent of its mother, shall be guilty of felony, to wit, of child destruction, and shall be liable on conviction thereof on indictment to penal servitude for life:

Provided that no person shall be found guilty of an offence under this section unless it is proved that the act which caused the death of the child was not done in good faith for the purpose only of preserving the life of the mother.'

The Act implies that if a woman has been pregnant for 28 weeks or more, this will be *prima facie* proof that she was at the time pregnant with a child capable of being born alive. Ms. Davison stated that this is the first time any law spells out a definition of 'child capable of being born alive'. The 1861 Offences Against the Person Act protected the child in the womb and the law on murder and infanticide protected the child after birth. The one situation where the child was not protected was in the actual process of being born.

Ms. Davison stressed that this Act was passed to amend the law regarding the destruction of children *at or before birth*. The inclusion of the words 'at or before birth' created an overlap with the 1861 Act which protected the child in the womb. In this sense, she said, the 1929 Act created a defence to child destruction, something that the 1861 Act did not do. The Act makes no mention of whether or not it is lawful to destroy a foetus under 28 weeks; it is only prohibited if over 28 weeks, with the exception contained in the proviso.

Ms. Davison remarked:

'It takes a lot of convoluted thinking to work this one out. Here is a defence in this Act if you want to carry out an abortion after 28 weeks, which is very strange because obviously there would be very few abortions you would want to carry out at such a late stage. But here you have a defence if you are doing that, if you can prove that it was done in good faith to preserve the life of the mother.'

In summary, it was said that under statute abortion law in Northern Ireland it appears that abortions are illegal under the 1861 Act, except in lawful cases (because the Act only talks about the unlawful situation), and that means those done in accordance with common law, which is, when necessary to save the life of the mother. The other exceptions to these prohibitions are the conditions introduced in the 1929 Act which overlap with the 1861 Act and in addition permit abortions on foetuses over 28 weeks if done in good faith to preserve the life of the mother.

The Bourne Judgment

It can be seen from the above that the law under which the medical profession had to operate in the post-1929 era after introduction of the Infant Life (Preservation) Act was a very confused and unsatisfactory one, unclear and ambiguous. Dr. Alex Bourne was a distinguished gynaecologist who, deliberately challenging the law in order to clarify affairs, in 1938 presented himself to the police and prosecution on confession that he had carried out an abortion on a 14 year old girl who had been the victim of a multiple rape by soldiers. With the consent of her parents, he carried out the operation, then reported himself and was arrested and consequently charged.

Dr. Bourne pleaded not guilty and brought medical evidence that if this young 14 year old girl had been forced to continue with the pregnancy, she would have become a mental and physical wreck. The judge was very sympathetic and in summing up to the jury, he interpreted the law in a very liberal way that helped secure Dr. Alex Bourne's acquittal. Having restated that the law allows termination of a pregnancy for preserving the life of the mother, Judge McNaghton continued:

> 'I think those words ought to be construed in a reasonable sense and, if the doctor is of the opinion on reasonable grounds and with adequate knowledge of the probable consequences, that continuing the pregnancy would be to make the woman a physical or mental wreck, the jury are quite entitled to take the view that the doctor who, under those circumstances and in that honest belief, operates is operating for the purpose of preserving the life of the mother.'

Ms. Davison stressed that this case is of major significance in that it extended the grounds for a lawful abortion to include the mental and physical well-being of the woman.

As a result of the Bourne decision, from 1938 onwards the medical profession had wider legal grounds, albeit limited, on which to perform hospital abortions. But one problem with the decision in the Alex Bourne case and McNaghton's judgment was that it was expressed in a court of first instance, that is, a lower court. Since Bourne was acquitted, the decision was never challenged before higher courts, such as the Court of Appeal or the House of Lords. If a pronouncement had been made by the latter courts, it would have become of much greater force.

The Legal Situation in Northern Ireland

Ms. Davison added that the situation in Northern Ireland currently, where there has been no equivalent of the Bourne judgment to clarify our version of the Infant Life (Preservation) Act, the Criminal Justice (Northern Ireland) Act, is as confusing as it was in England before 1938. As a result, doctors here tend to act extremely cautiously when it comes to abortion, at most going by common law rules and conducting abortions to save the life of the mother. Ms. Davison reported that, when conducting research on the subject in 1983, she had visited *the* top medic in Northern Ireland. This person, whom she did not want to name, had reported to her that the practice of the law in Northern Ireland was such that abortions are only performed for maternal and foetal indications, that is, where there is a serious risk to health or life. She was also informed at the time that more than half the women seeking abortions in Northern Ireland were refused, that the abortions performed are done only in the first three to five months, and that these amount to approximately 100 every year. Ms. Davison stressed that as the interview took place four years ago, the figure given is probably an understatement. When asked if backstreet abortions featured for subsequent treatment, the figure given to her was that of 250 curettages for incomplete abortions. Ms. Davison pointed out that this figure would not be backstreet abortions only, as she imagined women who miscarry spontaneously to be included. She also presumed that the person she spoke to might have erred on the side of caution, and that therefore the real figure could have been notably higher.

In conclusion, Ms. Davison said that, given the continuing legal ambiguity in which the medical profession in Northern Ireland has to operate, it might have been expected that the Department of Health and Social Services would have drawn up guidelines for doctors. It did not do so until the 1980s. However, with or without such guidelines, the fact remains, as she put it, that 'if anything, doctors err on the side of caution.'

The European Dimension

In reply to questions from panel members following her talk, Ms. Davison spent a little time looking at the European dimension. She pointed out that in 1981 there was a debate in the European Parliament, at the end of which the recommendation was made that women from member states should not need to make journeys across borders to obtain abortions; they should be able to find those facilities in their own country (see Box 6.4). Admittedly this recommendation had not the force of legislation, but it was still an important decision.

'The European Parliament ... notes that the relevant legislation in member states varies so widely that women in distress frequently have to seek help in other countries, and requests the Commission to press the Council for decisions at national level such as to obviate the need for journeys of this type which make any form of social aid impossible and lead to unacceptable commercialisation, and to ensure that every woman who finds herself in difficulty can obtain the necessary assistance in her own country.'

The Position of Women in the European Community , European Parliamentary Debate, Luxembourg, June 1981, pages 267-8.

The Republic of Ireland is also a member of the European Community. As such, the European Parliament's wish is directed at that state also, a point not lost on the Republic's representatives during the debate. They were angered by the contradiction of being members of a Parliament passing such a recommendation while at the same time representatives of a state whose law (and later Constitution) bans abortion.

A further constitutional dilemma for the Republic would be raised if the North were successful in obtaining the extension of the 1967 Abortion Act, or its equivalent (see Box 6.5).

Box 6.5

Abortion and the Constitution of the Republic of Ireland

As Open Line Counselling, the Dublin-based referral agency, pointed out in their evidence to the Tribunal, Articles 2 and 3 of the Republic's Constitution lay territorial claim to Northern Ireland. The relevant Articles are as follows:

Article 2: 'The national territory consists of the whole island of Ireland, its islands and the territorial seas.'

Article 3: 'Pending the re-integration of the national territory, and without prejudice to the right of the Parliament and Government established by this Constitution to exercise jurisdiction over the whole of that territory, the laws enacted by that Parliament shall have the like area and extent of application as the laws of Saorstat Eireann and the like extra-territorial effect.'

Article 40.3.3 of the same Constitution prohibits abortion as an interference with the guarantee of life to the unborn. How would this coexist with legislation in the North allowing abortion?

In relation to the Single European Act, she continued, it may transpire that the EEC decides to legislate in some way for health provisions. In that case, 'health' could be translated in a broad way to include the right to have an abortion.

Ms. Davison stated that one further element of this European aspect was the European Convention on Human Rights. A challenge could be mounted via that channel, as has already been successfully done in Northern Ireland in relation to the law on homosexuality. But there is one difficulty in relation to the Convention on Human Rights; you have got to have a victim. Taking a case to Europe is a lengthy, drawn-out and expensive process, but it certainly is fertile ground for consideration (see Box 6.6).

Box 6.6
International Dimensions of Abortion Law Reform

The International Tribunal organisers invited Rebecca J. Cook, Assistant Professor of Law at the University of Toronto, to attend the Tribunal. She was unable to do so, but sent a letter with some legal advice. Part of what she had to say ties in exactly with Madge Davison's conclusions.

'You might want to bring the attention of the Tribunal to the following points about the continued exclusion of Northern Ireland from the terms of the Abortion Act 1967:

1. Women's limited access to safe reproductive health care in Northern Ireland is not in keeping with international trends to ensure women's access to quality reproductive care.

(See "A Decade of International Change in Abortion Law: 1967-1977", *AJPH*, July 1978, vol. 68, No. 7.)

2. Britain, in denying women of Northern Ireland access to abortion, is not keeping pace with legal developments in the Commonwealth to ensure women the necessary services to reduce high rates of maternal mortality and morbidity.

(See "Modern Medical Technologies in Commonwealth Law and Beyond', *International Planned Parenthood Federation Medical Bulletin*, Vol. 17, No. 4, August 1983, and *Issues in Reproductive Health Law in the Commonwealth*, Commonwealth Secretariat).

3. Britain might be in violation of the European Convention of Human Rights by denying women of Northern Ireland, but not other British women, access to reproductive health services. In so doing Britain is exposing women of Northern Ireland to higher rates of maternal mortality and morbidity.

(See *The Human Right to Family Planning*, International Planned Parenthood Federation).

4. Britain might well be in violation of their obligations under the Convention on the Elimination of All Forms of Discrimination Against Women to ensure women on a basis of equality with men access to health care and to establish their families.

(See "Comment, The United Nations Convention on the Rights of Women: Opportunities for Family Planning Providers", *International Family Planning Perspectives*).'

7.

Medical Evidence

Introduction

As is clear from the previous chapter, there is severe legal ambiguity in relation to abortion in Northern Ireland. Given that, doctors are operating in a legal grey area when it comes to abortions. Certain consequences for medical practice follow, as will be made clear in this chapter, namely:

1. while there is clearly a need for abortion in Northern Ireland, the fact is that many are not performed which, legal ambiguities aside, would otherwise be performed;

2. tried and tested medical advances in relation to antenatal screening, particularly in relation to congenital abnormalities, are not being made available to women in Northern Ireland because of the lack of abortion locally.

We begin by looking at the guidelines provided by the Department of Health and Social Services to doctors in Northern Ireland who may be having to make decisions about abortion.

Guidelines on Abortion for Doctors in Northern Ireland

In Britain detailed notification of a termination of pregnancy is required, giving details of the doctors concerned, the reason for the termination and the place where the operation is to be performed. In Northern Ireland no such notification is mandatory, but in view of the uncertainty of the law relating to abortion in Northern Ireland, doctors are given guidelines as to how to act in such a situation. These guidelines have no basis in law. They are as follows:

1. All doctors concerned with possible terminations of pregnancy should be cautious in their attitude to abortion especially where there are no good medical indications.

2. All terminations should be agreed upon by at least two doctors, one of whom is a consultant gynaecologist.

3. All terminations should be performed in a National Health hospital.

4. No fee should be charged for termination of pregnancy.

Doctors are advised that

> 'if these suggestions are followed, it is very unlikely that the good faith of a doctor terminating a pregnancy would be questioned or legal action taken against him under the Act.'

Prenatal Diagnosis and Selective Abortion: A Consultant Medical Geneticist's Evidence

This is the legal advice to doctors. The question which follows is how such advice translates into action. First and foremost, the Tribunal was interested in how the absence of abortion locally affected prenatal diagnosis and care, especially in relation to congenital abnormalities in the foetus. Evidence in this regard was provided firstly by Professor Norman C. Nevin, Consultant Medical Geneticist.

Although unavailable to attend in person, Professor Nevin submitted written evidence to the Tribunal. He began by stating that since 1959, with the introduction of transabdominal amniocentesis, prenatal diagnosis and selective abortion have been a reality. At present several techniques are available which enable the diagnosis of serious congenital abnormalities to be carried out prenatally with a high degree of reliability. These techniques include:

ultrasonography,
transabdominal amniocentesis,
fetal blood sampling, and
fetoscopy and chorion villus biopsy (see Box 7.1).

Box 7.1
Glossary of Prenatal Diagnostic Techniques

Ultrasonography: using sound waves to create a visual picture of the foetus in the womb.

Transabdominal amniocentesis: a needle is inserted through the abdominal wall into the uterine cavity to withdraw amniotic fluid. Amniocentesis carries a risk of 1% spontaneous abortion of what may be a perfectly normal foetus. Most people in Britain consider it quite medically wrong to carry out an amniocentesis before sixteen weeks because of the much higher rate of miscarriage—there is not much amniotic fluid then—and because of the much higher rate of failure to grow the culture.

Foetal blood sampling: obtaining blood from the foetus by using a needle and syringe under ultrasound monitoring.

Chorion villus biopsy: a method of obtaining early information about the genetic make up of the foetus to identify abnormal genes. An instrument is passed through the neck of the womb to take a sample of

---

the tissues surrounding and nourishing the foetus before the placenta develops. This technique is still experimental and it is not known exactly how many women will lose their pregnancies as a result of the test. A randomised trial is being carried out in Britain in which for the first time the women have been involved in the planning, before the test is imposed upon a whole group of pregnant women.

In addition, new developments at St. Bartholomew's Medical College in London are expected to materialise into a new test offered to women. The test, which is for Down's Syndrome, tests the blood of pregnant women for a chemical called estriol which the foetus produces and is unusually low in the maternal blood of affected pregnancies. The test could detect up to 45% of such pregnancies without adding much to the cost of antenatal testing and is thought to be a much better screening test than alphafetoprotein.

Professor Nevin submitted that in counselling of couples and families with genetic disorders and congenital abnormalities, where the risk of recurrence of another affected child is increased, prenatal diagnosis may be the only way that some can confidently embark on a further pregnancy.

Ultrasonography between the fourteenth and eighteenth week of pregnancy can be used to detect serious structural abnormalities in the foetus. These abnormalities include anenecephaly, hydrocephalus, spina bifida, renal abnormalities and congenital heart disease (see Box 7.2). Transabdominal amniocentesis with culture of the amniotic fluid cells can be used to diagnose chromosomal abnormalities in the foetus at fifteen to eighteen weeks of pregnancy. This approach is extremely helpful in mothers over the age of 35 years, parents who are carriers for chromosomal rearrangements and in parents who have had a previous child with a chromosomal abnormality. Amniocentesis is also the investigation used to diagnose inherited metabolic disorders such as mucopolysaccharidosis and also 'open' neural tube defects such as spina bifida and anenecephaly.

Box 7.2

Glossary of Congenital Abnormality

Anenecephaly: failure of the development of the brain.

Hydrocephalus: distension of brain where fluid accumulates within the brain.

Spina bifida: where the neural tissue of the skin and muscle has not fused in the lower back. In the United Kingdom, 17 out of 100 such children live to be teenagers.

With the development of chorion villus biopsy, prenatal investigation can be carried out between 8 and 10 weeks of pregnancy, enabling selective abortion to be done at 10 to 12 weeks. Using DNA probes and chorion villus biopsy it is now possible to recognise gene disorders in the foetus at an early stage in pregnancy. These disorders at present include cystic fibrosis of the pancreas (affects 1 in 2000 live births), Duchenne muscular dystrophy (affects 1 in 3000 male births) and several other rare gene disorders such as tuberous sclerosis and myotonic dystrophy.

Professor Nevin submitted that an estimated 5% of antenatal patients could benefit from the availability of prenatal diagnosis. In Northern Ireland approximately 450 transabdominal amniocenteses are undertaken each year and, as a result, about 16 to 20 pregnancies are terminated. Ultrasonography is much more extensively used in antenatal clinics, but it is not possible to obtain an accurate figure of the number of pregnancies terminated as there is no established method for notifying terminations for abnormality in the foetus. Professor Nevin's own estimate was that between 35 and 40 pregnancies per year are terminated because of serious structural abnormalities detected by ultrasound.

Screening of antenatal patients with maternal serum alphafetoprotein (MSAF) is not routinely carried out in Northern Ireland because of the unavailability of abortion of pregnancy for abnormality. Maternal serum alphafetoprotein screening can be used to screen mothers who may be at risk of having an infant with an 'open' neural tube defect. Mothers, at 16-18 weeks gestation, with raised levels of maternal alphafetoprotein, can be further examined by ultrasonography and/or amniocentesis to confirm the diagnosis. Professor Nevin believed that this method of prenatal screening would be invaluable in Northern Ireland, a region which has the highest incidence of neural tube defects in the world (2.5 per 1000 total births). Maternal serum alphafetoprotein screening may also be used to screen mothers who may be carrying a foetus with Down's syndrome. In this situation the maternal serum alphafetoprotein is low in mothers at risk. Again Professor Nevin believed that this approach would be most helpful in Northern Ireland where the number of 'elderly' mothers is greater than elsewhere in the United Kingdom; for example, in Northern Ireland some 4% of mothers over the age of 40 years are pregnant compared with 1% in the rest of the United Kingdom.

Although generally opposed to abortion at a personal level, Professor Nevin concluded that there is a need for clarification of the legal situation of abortion in Northern Ireland for pregnancies in which the foetus has a serious congenital abnormality or a genetic disease. At present, abortion is carried out for such abnormalities detected by amniocentesis and ultrasonography. However, the numbers of abortions is small. The general unavailability of abortion for congenital abnormality in the foetus has prevented the introduction in Northern Ireland of screening procedures to detect spina bifida and Down's syndrome. Such procedures are available elsewhere in the United

Kingdom and would permit more women and their families in Northern Ireland to benefit from the advances which are taking place in prenatal diagnosis. (see Box 7.3).

Box 7.3

The Baird Report on Infant Mortality and Handicap

Confirmation for Professor Nevin's conclusion can be found in the Baird Report *You and Your Baby: Report of the Advisory Committee on Infant Mortality and Handicap in Northern Ireland* , Belfast, HMSO, 1980). The Report urged that genetic screening as a preventive measure be developed as soon as possible.

'Congenital abnormalities account for at least 30% of infant deaths and for a significant proportion of mental and physical handicaps in children. Many genetic disorders are serious and, with few exceptions, there is no effective treatment. Thus the only approach to such conditions is prevention. Many techniques are available already which could substantially reduce this burden of disease. These techniques include genetic counselling, genetic screening, carrier detection and prenatal diagnosis with selective termination of pregnancy.'

Despite such high-powered advice, no fundamental changes have occurred in the eight years since the Baird Report was published.

More recently, a multidisciplinary committee chaired by Professor Alwyn Smith and sponsored by the Health Education Authority in Britain, King Edwards Hospital Fund for London, the London School of Hygeine and Tropical Medicine and the Scottish Health Education Group, looked at the benefits of the 1967 Abortion Act. Their report, titled *The Nation's Health: a Strategy for the 1990s* recommended (on page 253) that 'the 1967 Abortion Act should be maintained and extended to Northern Ireland'.

The Lack of Routine Screening: Women's Experience

That routine screening, as advised by both Professor Nevin and the Baird Report, is needed in Northern Ireland is proven by statistical information made available to the panel. As Table 7.1 shows, spina bifida is much more common in Northern Ireland than in the rest of the United Kingdom. Moreover, mortality from congenital handicaps in the first year of life is twice as high in Northern Ireland as in EEC countries like France and the Netherlands.

Table 7.1: *Spina Bifida Births per 1,000 Live Births, 1978-83.*

	LIVE BIRTHS		STILL BIRTHS	
	NORTHERN IRELAND	ENGLAND AND WALES	NORTHERN IRELAND	ENGLAND AND WALES
1978	2.7	1.1	40.3	34.5
1979	2.4	1.1	74.8	32.4
1980	1.8	0.9	65.6	32.1
1981	1.9	0.8	75.3	29.5
1982	1.9	0.7	61.2	22.3
1983	1.5	0.6	36.1	13.5

Source: *Hansard,* Written Answers, 7 May, 1987.

However, that such routine testing was not freely available, despite the obvious need, in Northern Ireland was underlined by the testimony of two women to the Tribunal.

The first woman spoke from the floor on her experience of asking for the alphafetoprotein test.

'I asked for the alphafetoprotein test and the doctor in the City (Hospital) refused and, when I pressed my point, he said: "You know why you can't have it?", and I said, "Why?", and he said, "Because we don't have an Abortion Act here." And I said, "But women still have the right to have the test." So he wouldn't do anything else about it. I wrote to the head of the Eastern Health and Social Services Board and he eventually wrote back and said that for moral and ethical reasons the hospital does not give out the test, but that if women ask for it, if they knew about that, then they would be allowed to have it. So he arranged for me to have it. In fact, a very senior registrar at the hospital immediately phoned me up at work and was very concerned that I had been refused. I don't think that they wanted it to come out generally but they didn't want me to make more of an issue of it.'

The second woman (we will call her Jane) gave more lengthy evidence to the Tribunal.

Jane is 34 years old with a risk of spina bifida in the family. She had not been offered any form of screening voluntarily but, when she requested it, had found her own GP sympathetic, as was the hospital to which she was referred. She was offered a scan at fourteen weeks and a scan and amniocentesis at sixteen and a half weeks and counselled as to the risk of having amniocentesis. However she was not offered an alphafetoprotein test, although she had requested it.

She decided to have an amniocentesis which tested for Down's Syndrome and spina bifida. The results of the first test took four weeks to materialise, which meant that she was already over the limit of eighteen weeks. If the Alton Bill had been in operation this would have meant that the option of having an abortion would have been denied. The second test came through after six weeks when the woman was well over 22 weeks pregnant.

'I must emphasise that the staff of the hospital were aware of that problem and, as soon as the results were through, I was phoned at work. It just seems that there is no quicker way of doing it by the method that is available in Northern Ireland, namely amniocentesis and the culturing of cells. Looking at the other aspect, why I would be very, very annoyed, to put it mildly, if the eighteen week limit was imposed, although a lot of help appears to be offered in support of people with handicapped members of their family, it's very hard to come by in actual fact. Things like invalid care allowance have only just been introduced in Northern Ireland for married women within the last year; things like mobility allowance and attendance allowance may initially be awarded to a handicapped child but let me tell you, the benefits are soon taken away from the person. There are tests at the age of eight and fourteen and, even if the condition has got worse, not better, the financial support is withdrawn and it is very hard to appeal that decision. So if someone goes into a pregnancy expecting to have a lot of financial or community support, they can forget it. I don't think it's because people do not wish to give it but because of financial restrictions and the present government's attitude to caring in the community. They want the care in the community but they are not prepared to support it.'

Jane concluded that

'personally, I am not in favour of abortion as a means of contraception, but I am in favour of abortion as a means of choice for someone who may have a handicapped baby. That's the standpoint I'm taking. With that in mind and discussing it with my husband we, because of our family situation, would have gone through with an abortion. I was never given definite information as to where that would be carried out but it was implied that it would be.'

Under questioning by panel members after her submission, Jane stated that she was not told why the alphafetaprotein test was not available.

'They just said that they didn't do that. Having read the literature, it would have made my decision based on more fact had I had two tests to compare rather than one, as it's better to go through a less invasive test first; so I would have appreciated having an alphafetaprotein test.'

The ultimate insult in the procedure, from Jane's point of view, was that she was freely offered amniocentesis. The alphafetaprotein test

'would have caused no risk to the foetus or myself—whereas I was warned that there would be a 2 to 3 percent risk of abortion from an amniocentesis.'

Panel members were also interested as to why Jane had experienced such a long delay in getting the results of her tests.

'Unfortunately it was our July holidays in Northern Ireland; my pregnancy happened to come in that period, so ... The result hadn't come through. Once it had come through there was a very efficient method of letting mothers know but it takes a certain amount of time for the tests to be completed, for the cells to grow.'

Commenting on this delay Dr. Wendy Savage explained that the technical side of testing could not be slowed down and that it would normally take three weeks for the culture to grow, four weeks at the outside in a slow-growing culture. The failure to communicate the results until five to six weeks after the test was therefore not a medical problem, but must have been an administrative problem either because of financial restraints within the National Health Service or simply people back-peddling when they do not want to take part in the procedure.

Dr. Wendy Savage went on to say:

'It's part of this whole argument about who decides about the services provided. I understand that many women get ultrasound scans because the doctor thinks he needs to know when the baby's due, because he doesn't believe when the woman's last period was or when she said she got pregnant. Now the money that is put into the ultrasound scan, if women had a choice, could be diverted to be put into expanding the prenatal service.'

Doctors and Abortion in Northern Ireland: A General Practitioner's Evidence

Doctor G. Lundy, a General Practitioner working in the Twinbrook and Poleglass areas of Belfast, provided valuable evidence to the Tribunal based on 8 years experience as a GP. He began by giving a brief account of his work and the area in which it takes place.

Twinbrook and Poleglass have taken some of the overspill from West Belfast and transplanted some of the problems that are associated with the inner city. Dr. Lundy is in a group practice with three other doctors, and the practice has 5000 patients. Because it is such a new area, 40% of the patients are under 12 years of age—almost like a Third World country.

'Women stoically endure lives in those areas that are impoverished of resources and outlets in what can be a crippling and very doctrinaire community. Advice about termination of pregnancy is, therefore, because of this community perception, not common—even for those at high risk of foetal abnormality. On average I would see eight women per year who seek help, about half of these because of varying degrees of foetal risks. This is either due to drugs taken in the first three months of pregnancy or because of previous congenital abnormalities or infections. This group appear to get a lot of support and very sympathetic handling, with early consultant involvement to iron out any bureaucratic or nursing resistance. The community also are supportive.'

There is, according to Dr. Lundy, a second group of women, those seeking termination on physical, pychiatric or social grounds. These women can be treated very differently from the first group. To prove the point, he cited the case of a woman whom he called Mary; Mary had given unqualified approval to her case being presented to the Tribunal.

'Mary lives in Twinbrook. She is 26 years old and has four children—two boys and two girls, aged 7, 5, 3 and 1—and presented first when she was 11 weeks pregnant. Mary was one of 12 children and, because of a congenital heart defect, appeared to be very over-protected by the rest of the family. I came to know her quite well after the birth of her last baby when she presented with what was her usual complaint, frequent urinary infections. More worrying were bouts of acute anxiety and depression. My concern grew; her marriage was already floundering. Because I was out of my depth, I referred Mary to a psychiatrist who agreed generally with my own assessment. Mary couldn't cope with the four children and the constant warring that was going on with the husband. She had limited resources to cope with all these pressures. She had low self-esteem, lack of confidence and I felt that the prognosis was fairly poor.

This picture of this harassed woman working under pressure with four young children, with a relationship that was actually draining her must be a very common picture to anyone who works among women in parts of Belfast. Mary had decided on a termination. What I like to try and do, at that stage, is to send women to a woman whom they can talk things out with and I have found the Family Planning Association a very good place for this counselling to take place.

At the first consultation, I referred Mary through a telephone conversation with a Senior Registrar, who seemed to be sending positive vibes, and after ten days Mary returned to me and said that she had been seen at the hospital on two occasions and that what was needed was a psychiatric opinion before the obstetrician would move.

I tried all the hospitals in the immediate area—Downshire, Hollywell, Purdysburn, Windsor House. Even though the consultants were very polite and sympathetic, they could not help me on what they saw as ethical grounds. So that avenue to me was exhausted. However, there was still Mary's physical state. In previous pregnancies she had had a very severe kidney infection and actually required intravenous antibiotics, which is unusual. She also suffered from a congenital heart defect. I again got in contact with the hospital to which she had been referred and talked to her consultant. The consultant told me that Mary's physical state was adequate and would not be worsened by pregnancy. So much for that. Full stop. That was blocked. So I referred Mary back to my friend in the Family Planning Association. However because of money and what would be an unexplained absence, she decided to go on ahead with the pregnancy. Mary eventually had her baby, a girl of five pounds four ounces and required two admissions with severe kidney infections and is now getting by on intermittent courses of tranquilisers, even though I am totally against their use except in very rare cases.

The problems of working class women on income supplement or benefit to pay for their terminations, the price of isolation, the condemnation, the loneliness are very difficult to imagine. Society seems to want to punish them and they take it all alone. I always thought that I was in medicine to treat people who were in need and, if you could judge a civilisation, it would be on how it dealt with those people in need. I don't think we treat women in this situation very well.'

After his submission, Dr. Lundy was questioned by the panel. This allowed him both to clarify and expand on the evidence he had just presented. Most interesting were his comments in relation to actual abortions taking place currently in Northern Ireland. He reiterated a point he had made earlier, that sections of the medical profession here were enabling some abortions to take place locally.

'I think that the previous speakers have said how difficult it might be because of risk of foetal abnormality. I found in my own experience that there are certain hospitals where it is not difficult to get a termination.'

Panel members thought that it might be a useful service to women to list the hospitals where those abortions were taking place. Dr. Lundy replied:

'There is a problem. The hospitals take a catchment area. Lagan Valley is probably the easiest place to get a termination, which is outside Lisburn. I think next in order would be the Ulster, then the Royal and the City Hospital would be on par and never in the Mater.'

Dr. Lundy emphasised that he was talking here about abortions in the case of the risk of foetal abnormality. As for other women seeking abortions, like Mary, on psychiatric or social grounds, he added:

'I think the state of the art here is that somebody who has a psychiatric condition will not get a termination.'

As well as commenting on current medical practice, Dr. Lundy had some informed predictions to make about medical reactions to any changes in the law, such as the extension of the 1967 Abortion Act.

'I think that if the law was changed here, I can't see the floodgates opening to a large scale because of the fabric of society in Northern Ireland.'

As for the medical profession, such legal changes would, he believed, undoubtedly meet with resistance. 'I think the vast majority of doctors would be resistant.' Given that, there would be practical problems involved in providing easily accessible abortion facilities. For a start, 'I think the nursing staff would certainly cause problems. There is certainly a lot of resistance from some nurses.' Moreover, he felt that if anyone got around to opening up a private abortion clinic, 'I think it is likely to go up in a puff of smoke. I really do think that you are dealing with strange people here.'

On the other hand, Dr. Lundy was determined to end on a positive note, arguing that, despite inevitable resistance, legal change would be valuable not only for women but also for the medical profession. Legal change, such as the extension of the 1967 Act, 'would leave room for those people who may be on the fence to say, "All right I have now the legal framework in which I can follow my beliefs."

Evidence of Dr. C. Evans, General Practitioner

Medical evidence was next presented by GP Dr. Carole Evans. She comes from a working class practise outside of Belfast, a practise of under 3,000 people, of whom as many as 60% may be unemployed. Dr. Evans said that on average between four and six women would attend each year with an unwanted pregnancy which they were seriously contemplating having terminated. Most of these would be young and unmarried, but this would not exclusively be the case. Some very much older women were finding themselves with an unwanted pregnancy. Dr. Evans explained that all these women were usually very distressed and many of them had to overcome a great deal of social prejudice around them if they contemplated termination.

Because of the abortion legislation in Northern Ireland, nearly all of these women had to proceed to England if they decided to go ahead with a termination. this 'hurdle' of going away to England, and all the associated financial, travel problems, *etc*, made the problem several times harder for women from Northern Ireland. The thought of undertaking this amount of hassle, raising funds *etc* was enough to put some women off all together, and Dr. Evans pointed out that a number of women did not proceed with termination either because they could not face the added difficulties of going away and/or the problem of raising the money. Some then ended up reluctantly proceeding with the pregnancy. These women were more likely to seek out illegal (and highly dangerous) abortions, attempt to induce miscarriage in themselves, or in some (but certainly not all) cases to have an unhappy pregnancy and an unloved child.

Dr. Evans said that the UPAA provided a crucial and most helpful link to areas like hers and were most helpful to women.

Over the past ten years, Dr. Evans recounted, consultants in Northern Ireland and in the local hospital in particular have agreed to carry out a very few abortions. The policy on this was not uniform and very few women had been terminated in this way. All of these fell in some way into the category of legal abortions in Northern Ireland. Dr. Evans pointed out though that even then there were serious difficulties, not least the fact that some nursing and medical staff in the hospital who are morally opposed to abortion may opt to have the minimum or indeed nothing to do with any patient undergoing a termination. This could make the process very difficult and upsetting for a woman in hospital and could even mean, for example, that the termination took longer if it was dependent on hourly dosage regimes, *etc.*

When asked about the availability of contraception, Dr. Evans said that she thought that this situation was improving, but that there still is surprising ignorance amongst young people amidst such apparent sophistication. She felt that young men opted out since the days of the pill, taking the line that it is up to the girls, and that many young girls are still shy and concerned about being 'morally berated' for asking for the pill. Dr. Evans expressed a view that in some circles abortion is too easily used as a fall-back method of contraception, usually in the more educated (and well-off) women, and stated her disagreement. Dr. Savage sharply disagreed with Dr. Evans on this.

'It is a standard line of the anti-abortionists that abortion is used as a method of contraception. In my experience, women do not use abortion as a method of contraception. Women always find it a difficult decision to make but often by the time they get to the person who is going to do it or the nurses in the ward, those agonies have been gone through and they may well put a brave face on it. What I found in a study I did was that the women did not regret the decision to have an abortion; what they still regretted, five and seven years afterwards, was the act which had led them to get pregnant in the first place. Many women disapprove of abortion totally until they require it themselves or their daughter requires it or their granddaughter requires it and then suddenly it is different because they understand the situation. What we want is choice for women and that choice is based on having adequate education in the first place, which we don't have, adequate contraception, which we don't have, and a properly trained medical profession who are able to listen to what women want and not tell them what they, the doctors, think they ought to do.'

Like Dr. Lundy, Dr. Evans reached a positive conclusion, despite the pessimism instilled in the Tribunal as a result of her evidence. When asked what she thought would happen if the 1967 Act was extended to Northern Ireland, she replied:

'If the Act was introduced I think more doctors would refer patients and I think it would work to an extent. It would save people going away. Ideally you might be better off to have a special clinic in the province where people felt they could go and be treated decently without any stigma but I do think that if legislation were brought in there would be more and more GPs who would refer and there would be a number of consultants who would be prepared to go along with that and I think it could work.'

8.

The Abortion Tribunal: The Way Forward

Statement of Panel Members

At the close of the International Tribunal the panel members issued the following agreed statement:

'The 1967 Abortion Act was not extended to Northern Ireland, with the result that women in Northern Ireland facing an unwanted or accidental pregnancy are put in an unacceptable and disadvantaged position compared with women in the rest of the UK.

They are forced to endure the unwanted pregnancy, or make an expensive journey to England and pay for a private abortion, or undergo a backstreet abortion.

Evidence heard by the Tribunal confirmed that Northern Irish women suffer enormous emotional and psychological distress and unacceptable financial burdens as a result of the lack of abortion provision in Northern Ireland. They are prey to isolation, condemnation, fear and loneliness, often in excess of women elswhere in the UK, owing to the social, cultural and religious complexity of their society.

The non-extension of the 1967 Abortion Act to Northern Ireland ensures that doctors in Northern Ireland have no clear guidelines as to whether to perform an abortion or not. The law remains ambiguous and results in serious inconsistencies in its application. Pregnancy as a result of rape or incest or in the case of severe risk to a woman's health do not guarantee an abortion. This situation underlines the necessity for an urgent change in the law.

According to legal, medical and individual evidence presented to the Tribunal, it is clear that serious double standards exist on the part of the medical profession in attitudes, information and services. In spite of this, evidence presented to the Tribunal suggests that up to 500 abortions are performed annually in Northern Ireland. But it appears that doctors are imposing their individual religious, moral and ethical judgements upon women. Furthermore, the ambiguity in the abortion law in Northern Ireland enables them to suspend their objective and professional judgement to carry out an abortion when it would be legitimate, under existing law.

Further evidence showed that the absence of provision for abortion and adequate pregnancy services discriminates against working class women in particular as a result of reduced economic and social circumstances.

Lack of abortion facilities in Northern Ireland has led to women being denied basic preventive medical care. Many medical authorities believe that, as a termination of pregnancy cannot be offered, then ante-natal testing for congenital deformity in the foetus is invariably pointless and unnecessarily traumatic. As a result, Northern Ireland suffers from a very high rate of spina bifida and other neural tube defects and the Tribunal believes this situation will continue as long as the 1967 Act is not extended to Northern Ireland.

The absence of the Act has forced at least 20,000 women from Northern Ireland to seek abortions in England since 1967.

The Tribunal draws your attention to the conclusions of the 1977 Lane Committee which found that in the ten years since the implementation of the Act,

"that the Act has relieved a vast amount of individual suffering. It has helped also to focus attention on the paramount need for preventive action, for more education in sexual life and its responsibilities, and for the widespread provision of contraceptive advice and facilities. It has served to stimulate research into all aspects of abortion and development of safer operative techniques. These have been undeniably great benefits."

The Tribunal therefore makes the following recommendations and believes that:

a woman should have the right to make a free decision about her own pregnancy;

women are the best judges of their own situation and all choices, including that of abortion on request should be available to them;

there should be comprehensive advice, information and sex education, contraceptive provision and ante/post-natal medical care available to all women in Northern Ireland.

In this respect we believe the UK government has an obligation to extend the 1967 Abortion Act to Northern Ireland.

The gains facilitated by extension of the Act would far outweigh any shortcomings for which it is criticised. Women in Northern Ireland should have at least the same rights as women in the rest of the UK. We believe the extension of the Act will reduce the unnecessary and inhumane suffering women in Northern Ireland are forced to endure through unwanted pregnancy. Advances in medical research will be more fully utilised in the protection and improvement of women's health in Northern Ireland.

We make these demands in the interests of all women in Northern Ireland and as the only responsible and humane response to this urgent problem. We believe the extension of the 1967 Abortion Act would promote better health and happiness in Northern Irish society.

Members of the Tribunal pledge their support for Northern Irish women in their struggle and campaign for a satisfactory legal basis for abortion services and will exploit the potential of international law in this respect. The Tribunal is of the opinion that a number of developments, *eg* in Sweden and other parts of the world, have provided a far more adequate legal basis to ensure the protection of women's right to control their fertility.'

In the closing public session of the Tribunal and in answering questions from the press, members of the Tribunal indicated the ways in which a campaign to implement its final recommendations might be pursued.

An extension of the 1967 Act to Northern Ireland would, it appears, currently be opposed by a large majority of the population. Consequently, Tribunal members directed their remarks to various issues concerning law and public opinion:

the nature of public opposition to abortion in Northern Ireland;

the use of law to change opinion;

how opinion in Northern Ireland and elsewhere might otherwise be changed;

how the law might be changed in defiance of stated opinion;

the nature of law itself;

and the possibility of defying the law on abortion.

Public opposition to abortion in Northern Ireland

First, it was disputed that opposition to abortion in Northern Ireland is as clear and unambivalent as suggested. The current situation, with its criminalisation of abortion and accompanying oppressive atmosphere, prevents many from speaking out on the subject. Wendy Savage reminded the audience that 20,000 women had travelled from Northern Ireland to England since 1967 to have abortions, and added that

'the experience of abortion [in Northern Ireland] is not really different from the experience of abortion in Britain—at the individual woman's level of having it. What is different is that she hasn't had the opportunity to have her abortion in a climate of support from her community'.

Sabine Klein-Schonnefeld commented that everywhere in Europe there is

'quite a big population of women who ... have taken the very, very hard decision to have an abortion ... [but] as long as this is criminalised they are not allowed to talk about it. They can't speak openly about it.'

An extension of the Act had perhaps the silent support of many women who would not speak openly about abortion. Thus, what was needed was for those women from Ireland who had had abortions to make a public declaration in support of extension. As Wendy Savage concluded,

> 'If all those women in Northern Ireland and Southern Ireland were to get together and say, "We want the law extended so that our daughters and our sisters can have abortions without the trauma that we went through", that would change the law ... But men are the ones who make the laws and men aren't the ones who have abortions. They merely cause the women to get pregnant.'

The use of law to change opinion

Secondly, it was argued that a change in the law might itself bring about a change in attitudes. Sabine Klein-Schonnefeld maintained that

> 'it was the case in the Netherlands that the social practice in respect to abortion came first and then the law was changed. Within the other European countries, especially Germany ... first of all the law was changed and then the attitudes changed.'

Kadar Asmal, describing the decriminalisation of homosexuality in Northern Ireland, pointed out that this took place, not 'out of the goodness of [the British Government's] heart' but rather 'because of external intervention'. Here, he said, was a 'classic example where the law was imposed notwithstanding virtually uniform opposition coming from the Churches [and] from most of the political parties'. There was evidence that attitudes had subsequently changed. Moreover, even if 'deep down people may still want to Save Ulster from Sodomy ... they can't do anything about it'. (See Box 8.1)

Box 8.1

ALRA's Statement on Abortion Law Reform

In their statement to the Tribunal, the Abortion Law Reform Association (ALRA) in Britain urged legal change as the way forward.

> 'Starting from virtually nothing, it could be argued that you have nothing to lose by using a Private Member's Bill, or one of the other ways of raising an issue in Parliament, such as a ten minute rule Bill. Many people in Great Britain are currently not even aware that the 1967 Abortion Act doesn't apply in Northern Ireland. A Private Member's Bill, taking up the question of extending the 1967 Abortion Act to Northern Ireland, would contribute to a consciousness-raising exercise in all the United Kingdom. It would allow all those who support the extension of the Act campaigning now in Northern Ireland to identify and asssess your support in Parliament—and then gradually build on it.

> Remember that ALRA had several unsuccessful attempts before actually getting a Bill through Parliament—but each attempt revealed growing support amongst the public, the media, the Protestant clergy and some members of the establishment.'

Of course, there is one way in which legal change could emerge more quickly, namely, through a Labour Party government committed to the current party manifesto coming to power. A letter from Labour Party Spokesperson on Northern Ireland, Peter Archer, reminded the Tribunal of this option.

'As Labour Party Spokesperson on Northern Ireland, I send warm greetings to those involved with the Tribunal and wish you the greatest possible success in the achievement of your aims. There can be little doubt that the failure to extend the provisions of the 1967 Abortion Act to Northern Ireland has very serious implications for any advocate of civil liberties. It is very commendable to see an event such as this taking place and discussing and analysing the problems created by such a situation.

Irrespective of the merits of the issue, the right to *choose* remains vital for all people and the fact that Northern Ireland is treated differently is clearly an infringement upon the civil liberties of its citizens. It is for this reason that the Labour Party remains committed to the extension of the 1967 Abortion Act and why it is contained within the Labour Party manifesto.'

How opinion in Northern Ireland might otherwise be changed

Thirdly, there remained many ways in which public opinion—in Northern Ireland and elsewhere—might be changed. The Tribunal itself would play its part in influencing people. 'We are from these islands and from Europe', said Kadar Asmal, 'and governments are sensitive to pressure.' He also stressed the important role of professional bodies and organisations in this pressure. Lucy Schmitz underlined this point by speaking about the Netherlands experience where the women's movement, doctors, judges and lawyers publicly stated their support for the provision of abortion facilities. This 'worked to influence public opinion and to influence parliament at the same time.'

Sarah Spencer pointed to the unfortunate ignorance in Britain of the situation in Northern Ireland:

'My experience in coming over here in telling people why I was coming was a sense of disbelief, and I found a lot of people who I would have expected to be quite well-informed simply didn't realise that the 67 Act didn't extend over here and were quite shocked. And I think that when I go back and tell them what I've actually learnt about what women go through ... it will be quite easy to raise public awareness and get the pressure on the government to change the law.'

84

Julie Grant promised to ensure that the issue of abortion was given 'an even higher profile' in the future within both the NUS and the USI. Work in colleges would mean that a lot more people, 'particularly in England where ... the ignorance about the situation in Northern Ireland is very high', became aware of the issues.

Carol Tongue promised as a Member of the European Parliament to make more of her parliamentary colleagues 'aware of the fact that the Act isn't extended here to Northern Ireland, and particularly women in the European Parliament.'

How the law might be changed in defiance of stated opinion

Fourthly, the Tribunal members pledged to assist NIALRA in exploring the various ways by which the law might be changed, regardless of public opinion. Sarah Spencer spoke of the possibility of using a Private Member's Bill at Westminster to secure an extension, and promised the help of the NCCL in pursuing such a parliamentary strategy.

Others spoke of the European dimension. Carol Tongue mentioned

'the UN Convention on Discrimination against Women ... we are at the moment looking ... very closely to find out where the United Kingdom Government is still violating its provisions'.'

The possibility of taking a case on abortion and Northern Ireland to the European Court of Human Rights was discussed, and the difficulties of such a strategy were outlined.

The nature of law itself

Fifthly, members of the Tribunal warned against taking a benign view of the law and its operation. Sabine Klein-Schonnefeld commented that 'law is not an objective thing and it depends on power and the power base.' She commented on the German experience where recently a woman with a German passport had been prosecuted in Germany for having an abortion in the Netherlands.

'So even if you go to another country where you can get a legal abortion under circumstances which you couldn't get, for instance in the south of Germany, and you come home again you can be prosecuted.'

The possibility of defying the law on abortion

Sixthly, the Tribunal members were asked if it might not be possible for doctors to come over from England to perform abortions in Northern Ireland. Wendy Savage commented:

'Maybe what we ought to do is to start a sort of weekend abortion service, because I worked out that, if you did 20 abortion operations a day, in a weekend you could do 40 operations. And if you charged the women £50 each, that would make enough to pay the fare and rent a place to do it—if we don't have to have an approved place. The only thing is that there's some 1984 Nursing Home Act. And then maybe you could have 10 doctors ... who come five times each in a year, and do it and then see what happens. Be interesting, wouldn't it? Because looking at the UPAA referrals, 40% of those come from GPs, so it seems that if you let the GPs know, the Family Planning and UPAA, you would immediately have a target population. If one had to rent a very expensive nursing home then it might have to be more than £50, but it certainly must be less than it would be if you flew over to England and had it done. So I think that might be an alternative strategy whilst we're getting the 1967 Act brought over to Northern Ireland.'

The Tribunal members were asked what might be the legal repercussions of trying to operate a private abortion clinic in Northern Ireland. Wendy Savage outlined her experience in New Zealand which provided an interesting parallel to the position in Northern Ireland.

'In New Zealand when I went in 1973 they started a day-care abortion service—a group of women and doctors. And the situation in New Zealand was as it is here. The 1967 Act didn't apply; they still had the 1861 Offences Against the Person Act and I think they had ILPA [Infant Life (Preservation) Act] as well. And so they started this abortion service, and there's a very powerful Catholic lobby in New Zealand—15% of the population are Catholic—but they seemed to be very over-represented in professions like medicine, law ... and in Parliament. And after a couple of years they raided the clinic, took away 300 sets of records—illegally of course—and then took the doctor who was doing the abortions to court where he was acquitted of doing illegal abortions. SPUC were not content with that. They then lobbied and finally got a Royal Commission set up into contraception, sterilisation, and abortion. And this was interesting. This is what made me become politically involved actually. Then what happened was that they packed the Committee with anti-abortion people and produced a very retrogressive report and then Parliament passed an extremely repressive law which the liberal doctors refused to take part in initially. And then the feminists flew all the women over to Australia to have abortions, because fortunately the Australians had changed their law and they could get them free. And then after a few years it sort of settled down and, although the law hasn't changed, the practice has changed so that women in New Zealand have perfectly reasonable access to abortion under this very bad law.

Suppose you set it up secretly—so that you didn't have a lot of publicity about it—you just told doctors and people that you thought you could trust, and then you started doing them. I don't know what would happen because this is a very repressive society, isn't it? And I should imagine the police would be there on the second weekend. But I don't know.'

From the floor Madge Davidson quoted the report produced by CREW (Centre for European Research into Women) concerning those European countries whose abortion practice was in defiance of the domestic law.

'You had private clinics operating, breaking the law every day of the week, performing abortions and, generally speaking, what was happening was that there were a few interventions by the police—not very often—because they were being allowed to do it. The law was turning a blind eye because the alternative was unthinkable—of arresting large numbers, depending on how many they got, of women and doctors, and prosecuting them. So the reality was the law didn't allow abortions but they were actually being performed on the ground and the authorities were turning a blind eye to it. I'm not saying that's what's going to happen here but one thing that would be very interesting would be just to see what would happen. Could we get our hands on enough doctors encouraged to do it? Because there is no way of making the law look an ass easier than by actually doing that. And I would very much doubt if you would see a number of prosecutions of doctors. I very much doubt it.'

Lucy Schmitz, however, cautioned against this approach. One, she said,

'should be very careful not to generalise these situations because actually in Belgium it is still prohibited to perform abortions. The police are .... rather active from time to time. So it is a very dangerous situation in Belgium for women and doctors to perform abortions. On the other hand, as far as the situation in the Netherlands is concerned, abortion was forbidden by the law. But at the same time there was some common law which gave the abortion clinics the possibility and the guarantee that they could work as they did. So it was quite different.'

Conclusion

In conclusion, the Northern Ireland Abortion Law Reform Association pledged that—whether it involved working to change public opinion in Northern Ireland and elswhere or securing a change in the law despiite public opposition—it would do everything within its means to secure an extension of the 1967 Abortion Act to Northern Ireland and thus implement the recommendations of the Tribunal. The Tribunal itself had been, added NIALRA, an important and significant step in 'breaking the silence' on abortion in Northern Ireland and bringing about the much needed change in the law.